Discover the True

Hawaiian Magic and Spirituality is the first book solely devoted to the spirituality of the Hawaiian people and how taboos, superstitions, and magical practices historically permeated and defined every aspect of their lives.

Celebrated author Scott Cunningham—who spent 20 years studying traditional Hawaiian culture—offers a historical and sociological perspective on the fascinating beliefs of Hawaiians before the advent of Christianity: the structure of its society of rulers, commoners, and slaves; the names and ways of the many major and minor deities; the practice of deifying ancestral spirits; the magical and religious importance of dance, colors, water, stone, and plants; and the underlying concept of *mana,* the Hawaiians' name for the spiritual power that pervades all things.

Learn about traditional Hawaiian methods of divination, reading omens, practicing magic, and predicting the future—and find out which of these traditions live on today.

The religion of the ancient Hawaiians was a rich, all-encompassing spirituality deeply rooted in the land, the wind, the rain, and the ocean. This wonderful book will introduce you to the true magic of Hawaii . . . and to a world unlike any other you've ever known.

About the Author

Scott Cunningham learned about Wicca while still in high school, and practiced elemental magic for twenty years. He was the author of more than forty books, both fiction and non-fiction, sixteen of them published by Llewellyn Publications. He experienced, researched, then wrote about what he learned in his magical training. Scott's books reflect a broad range of interests within the New Age sphere, where he was highly regarded. He passed from this life on March 28, 1993, after a long illness.

To Write to the Publisher

If you would like more information about this book, please write to Llewellyn Worldwide. The publisher appreciates hearing from you and learning of your enjoyment of this book and how it has helped you. Llewellyn Worldwide cannot guarantee that every letter written will be answered, but all will be reviewed. Please write to:

Llewellyn Worldwide
P.O. Box 64383, Dept. K188–0, St. Paul, MN 55164-0383, U.S.A.
Please enclosed a self-addressed, stamped envelope or $1.00 to cover costs.
If outside the U.S.A., enclose international postal reply coupon.

HAWAIIAN
MAGIC &
SPIRITUALITY

SCOTT
CUNNINGHAM

2000
Lewellyn Publications
Saint Paul, Minnesota 55164-0383, U.S.A.

SECOND EDITION
First Printing, 2000
(Previously titled *Hawaiian Religion and Magic)*
First edition published by Llewellyn Publications, 1994, two printings

Cover design: Anne Marie Garrison
Cover photo: Randy Braun/Hawaiian Art Photography
Photographs: Scott Cunningham
Book design and layout: Jessica Thoreson

ISBN 1-56718-188-0
Library of Congress Cataloging-in-Publication Data (Pending)

Llewellyn Publications
A Division of Llewellyn Worldwide, Ltd.
P.O. Box 64383, St. Paul, MN 55164-0383
www.llewellyn.com

Printed in the United States of America

This book is dedicated to the memory of
Mary Kawena Pukui

Acknowledgements

My deepest thanks to the following individuals who, directly or indirectly, assisted in the completion of this book: Ruthie Phillips, who first taught me the old traditions; Marilee for sharing many Hawaiian adventures with me; A. K. for opening the door into the *kahuna* philosophy; Ron and Sandy for putting me up and for insight into pre-missionary days in Hawai'i; Sally and Jerry for their gracious hospitality on O'ahu; the Jaggar Museum and the The Hawai'i Visitors Bureau.

All faults in interpreting and presenting the information in this book remain, of course, my own.

Other Books by the Author

Magical Herbalism
Earth Power
Cunningham's Encyclopedia of Magical Herbs
The Magical Household (with David Harrington)
Cunningham's Encyclopedia of Crystal, Gem, and Metal Magic
The Complete Book of Incense, Oils, and Brews
The Truth About Witchcraft Today
Wicca: A Guide for the Solitary Practitioner
Magical Aromatherapy: The Power of Scent
The Magic in Food
The Truth About Herb Magic
Earth, Air, Fire, and Water: More Techniques of Natural Magic
Spell Crafts: Creating Magical Objects (with David Harrington)
Living Wicca: A Further Guide for the Solitary Practitioner
Dreaming the Divine

Video

Herb Magic

Biography

Whispers of the Moon: A Biography of Scott Cunningham
(by David Harrington deTraci Regula)

Table of Contents

Linguistic Note

The Hawaiians lacked an alphabet when they met Westerners. Memory was used in place of writing to store geneologies, sacred stories ("myths"), technological applications, dances and songs, and magical and religious practices. Early missionaries attempted to fit the spoken Hawaiian language to our alphabet. Controversy still rages over whether the "k" sound should have been recorded as "t" and the "l" sound as "r" (as it is in Tahitian). Since this alphabet has been in use for well over 100 years, I've used these preferred spellings, as listed in the authority on the subject: *Hawaiian Dictionary* (Pukui and Elbert, 1986). Still, many Hawaiian sounds are nearly impossible to reproduce from the written words alone.

Stress is usually on the second to last syllable, but this is by no means universal. The consonants and vowels are basically pronounced:

p, k, h, l, m, n: Much like in English.

w: Following i and e, a "v" sound; following u or o, like the English "w;" following a or as the first letter of a word, like either "w" or "v."

a, e, i, o, u: Generally, vowels are pronounced much as in English, with many variants. (For pronunciation assistance, see *Hawaiian Dictionary,* pp. xvii-xviii.)

As an expert in Hawaiian language once told me, it's impossible to move Hawaiian into English without losing much of Hawaiian's integrity. This is true because Hawaiian is a rich, poetic language, and its speakers delighted (and still delight) in puns, double entendre, hidden meanings, and other word play. Though limited to just seven consonants and five vowels, Hawaiians arranged these few letters into an amazing variety of words. Even the 30,000 entries in the *Hawaiian Dictionary* can only begin to record this language's rich complexity.

This book's Hawaiian orthography (the method in which the language is presented in print) is somewhat singular. I've chosen to italicize nearly all Hawaiian words and terms, save for deity names, proper names of persons, islands, towns, cities, island districts, and places throughout Hawai'i. And though the use of hyphens is currently frowned upon by Hawaiian scholars and teachers, I've chosen to occasionally hyphenate long deity names (such as Hi'iaka-i-ka-poli-o-Pele) simply to assist those unfamiliar with Hawaiian. (I haven't altered bibliographic entries and exact quotes, so some exceptions to this can be found in this book.)

Additionally, I've used the glottal stop (represented by an apostrophe). This occurs between vowels in words which have, over the passing of time, lost a consonant. The sound represented by a glottal stop is similar to that between the ohs in "oh-oh."

I've chosen not to use the macron in this book for technical production reasons. The macron, which identifies the stressed syllable, is necessary in presenting Hawaiian to non-native speakers, as many words can be pronounced in two, three, or four ways with different stresses, and each can have radically different meanings. For example, *kahuna,* pronounced with stress on the first syllable, is singular; pronounced with stress on the second syllable, the word is plural.

Finally, Hawaiian is a rich language. Most Hawaiian words have many meanings, each shaded to give a different interpretation. Though I've included a Hawaiian glossary in this book, it is by no means authoritative, and lists definitions of Hawaiian words only within the parameters of their usage in this book.

Preface

Many books have been written about Hawai'i, from scholarly volumes to collections of folktales to wildly romantic fictions. Picture books, travel guides, histories, and sociological studies crowd the shelves. Mark Twain, Robert Louis Stevenson, Jack London, James A. Michener, and many other authors have devoted books and short stories to this subject. For over 150 years, Hawai'i has been a popular topic for authors from around the world.

Some of these works describe the luxuriant beauty of Hawai'i. Others discuss, to a degree, the peoples who once thrived there. There are accounts of missionaries and the diaries of other men and women who visited Hawai'i in the early 1800s. Archaeological records, analyses of myths, and accounts of Hawaiian ethnobotany and royalty can be found in abundance.

Surprisingly, though, no one book has provided an overview of traditional Hawaiian spirituality. It's this topic that we'll explore in this work. Since virtually every aspect of life in ancient Hawai'i was intimately related to religion, this is a vast subject, and many areas can only be touched upon here. The Bibliography leads to reliable sources of further information.

I've had many reasons for writing this book. First, I've spent 20 years studying traditional Hawaiian culture and the last 10 travelling throughout Hawai'i. Second, I've been appalled at some of the books that have been published in recent years that promise to teach the "secrets" of "Hawaiian magic" and deliver nothing. And finally, I've had no choice: like other writers before me, I've become enchanted with Hawai'i.

The words and pictures in this book are mere shadows of Hawai'i. Words can't capture the image of trembling aquamarine water lapping green and black sand beaches, the beauty of an emerald valley ringing with the cries of birds, the scents of exotic plants mixing with the ocean's salt, the sight of the sun painting the western horizon with fire, the power of explosive lava pouring into the ocean, or the low, humming peace experienced within rock-walled temples built century upon century ago.

Hawai'i truly is a world apart. This is a land of rain and deserts, innumerable waterfalls, red earth and blue skies, fertile fields and multi-colored canyons, healing stones and phallic rocks, sacred rivers and tabooed valleys, cinder cones, secret caves, volcanic hair, green cliffs, haunted woods, rainbow fish, fragrant flowers, coral reefs, blow holes, jeweled beaches, and live volcanoes.

This phantasmagorical setting gave birth to a culture unmatched in modes of spiritual expression and environmental concern. Glorious isolation produced a rich, multi-layered, all-encompassing spirituality deeply rooted in the land, the wind and rain and ocean.

In our ongoing quest to answer eternal questions, humans have always turned for assistance to religion (or to its less-structured form, spirituality). Hawaiians looked to their island world to answer their questions and, in doing so, came far closer to truth than have many other peoples.

And yet, just over 200 years after contact with the outside world, Hawai'i's fabulous culture and its original modes of spirituality are virtually unknown to the outside world.

What is known is generally incorrect or incomplete: the theories of Max Freedom Long's completely non-Hawaiian "Huna," the concept that all *kahuna* are evil, that Hawaiians tossed virgins into volcanoes, that the Hawaiians were ignorant and savage persons who surfed and danced but lacked science, philosophy, and true religion.

This, then, is another reason for this book: putting to bed such false notions and replacing them with fact.

The information contained within this work has been gathered from a number of sources. Some has generously been shared by the many cultural Hawaiians that I've known throughout my life. Much of it has been culled from early authoritative sources that were written either by Hawaiians or by specialists who recorded information from aging Hawaiians, many of whom heard stories of long-vanished times from their grandparents.

This book is rooted in fact, not wild speculation or romantic fantasy. Fortunately, truth is far more wondrous than fiction.

It is my fondest hope that this book will introduce you to the true magic of Hawai'i.

Me ke aloha,
SCOTT CUNNINGHAM
7/25/92

PART ONE

The People and
the Deities

Hawaiian greeting

CHAPTER ONE

The Land and the People

Try to imagine this: you've left your home. For weeks you've been at sea with your family and dozens of other people, surviving on little food and less water. The huge double outrigger canoe that has been your home rolls restlessly on the Pacific Ocean. Your navigator, following traditional information garnered from the stars, from ocean swells, clouds, birds, and other signs, has patiently guided your canoe, but the sea seems to have swallowed up all land.

Then, finally, a tell-tale mound of clouds rises on the horizon. You row faster toward the tantalizing speck of white. It grows. Eventually, verdant mountains appear through the clouds.

The sound of waves crashing against the coral reef echoes. The scent of fresh earth wafts toward you. Your canoe slices through the water. The navigator finds a break in the reef surrounding the island. A wave catches the canoe, lifting you higher and higher, propelling you toward the enticing land.

The island is larger than any you've ever seen: tall, laced with fantastic cliffs and sparkling waterfalls. This is what you've come for: this speck of land in the middle of the largest ocean on Earth.

3

Your navigator found the island by the use of an exact science. But the existence of the land is a gift from the deities. Every cliff, every tree, every river and beach and stone emanates spiritual energy.

So you revere the deities that led you to this island and set out to discover the new deities resident within it. For all islands—all land— were created by the gods and goddesses.

Your migration party settles down to living on the island. Soon others will join you, lured by the fertile valleys and abundant seas. You create a society, adapt skills, introduce new plants and animals to the island. But you never forget that first moment when island appeared before you; when the miracle of the existence of land amidst the vast ocean manifested. And this will be the basis of your religion: land.

Hawai'i was born of fire in the middle of the Pacific Ocean. Its main islands lie approximately 2,000 miles from the nearest continent. Originally, there were no islands of Hawai'i. A "hot spot" on the ocean's floor began pouring out lava. As each layer cooled on the sea floor, more molten rock flowed on top of it. Eventually, this seamount broke through the surface of the water. It continued to grow as yet more lava was sent to its surface, creating a massive island.

According to the theory of plate tectonics, the newly born island drifted to the north, away from the volcanically volatile area, allowing another island to be formed. This creative process continued until each of the Hawaiian islands had been created, and it continues today on the island of Hawai'i.

The shaping of Hawai'i had only begun. Moisture in the air, trapped by the enormous island volcanoes, poured rain onto the black lava peaks and carved them into mountain ranges. Life began to arrive: insects trapped in air currents, seeds deposited on the shores of the emerging beaches, birds blown off course during migrations. Coral reefs slowly built up on the submerged cliffs.

Above the ocean's reach, green carpeted the islands. Life took firm hold on these fertile places. Insect, bird, and plant species evolved to suit their new environment, creating unique forms unknown elsewhere in the world. Rains continued to erode the islands, altering their contours, while further south in the chain new islands were still being born.

Finally, in some unknown time (perhaps about 500 CE), humans from the South Pacific arrived on these blessed shores. Stepping from their outrigger canoes, these Polynesian explorers found the fertile islands to be suitable new homes. They lived a fairly simple lifestyle on the islands.

Then, in perhaps 1000 CE, a new wave of migrations from Polynesia (probably Tahiti) began. The newcomers came well equipped with food plants, baby pigs, chickens, dogs, and other necessities for survival. Their crafts were large outrigger canoes, capable of carrying supplies and as many as 60 people. With superior culture and technology, these newcomers vanquished the earlier inhabitants of Hawai'i, who soon all but disappeared.

For about 200 years, many voyages took place between Hawai'i and Tahiti. During this period, Hawaiian culture was heavily influenced by that of its ancestral home. Eventually, however, this period of intercourse ceased, and Hawaiians lived in total isolation. They evolved a magnificent culture rich in spirituality and rooted in the Earth. Their social system was strict and orderly.

For hundreds of years, Hawaiians lived in relative harmony. Ruling chiefs did indeed attack each other, and war was common, but even battles were ruled by religious strictures. Between the times of bloodshed and famine there were days of peace and plenty.

Anyone who's the least bit sensitive to place, on arriving in Hawai'i, senses the unusual atmosphere that emanates from the islands. It can't be seen and is difficult to describe, but this peaceful, humming energy is part of what convinces many visitors to return.

This energy seems to stem first from the land itself, then from the surrounding ocean and fresh water, and finally from the air. The residents—particularly cultural Hawaiians—also emanate this energy.

It can be felt when hiking a hanging, ferny valley. It can be sensed when walking along a lonely beach. It can be absorbed by eating locally-grown foods. This energy has been given a name: *mana* (spiritual power).

Why is Hawai'i's *mana* so different from that felt at other places on the globe? Why should these islands be so spiritually blessed, alive, and active?

The answers seem to lie in the comparatively recent (geologically speaking) creation of the islands, in their location in the middle of the sea, and in the many unique plants and birds that inhabit them. Hawaiians themselves might say that the deities doubly blessed the islands with power.

The *mana* of vulcanism, isolation, and endemic species blend to create an unusually strong form of spiritual power. *Mana* inhabits everything in the islands: the people, the rocks, the flowers, the springs, the ground itself. It is this vital energy that people miss when they leave Hawai'i, and that often calls them back for a repeat visit.

There are many beautiful tropical islands throughout the world, in both major oceans. None possesses Hawai'i's unique *mana*. If we as persons living in a hard-science world can feel the power of Hawai'i, is it any wonder that its earliest inhabitants deemed the islands sacred?

And so they were. All land on every island was owned by the *akua*, the gods and goddesses. Private ownership of land was forbidden. Chiefs were the caretakers of the land; the commoners worked it to provide food for all. This was the way it was: the islands belonged to the goddesses and gods.

A few words must be said here regarding the Hawaiian social system. A rigid class system was in use. This consisted of three classes: *ali'i*, *maka'ainana*, and *kauwa*.

The *ali'i* were the ruling, chiefly class. All who were born into this class were directly descended from the gods and goddesses, and ruled by divine right. Some chiefs were themselves considered to be *akua* (gods) during life or after death. The *ali'i* possessed enormous amounts of *mana* (spiritual power). The famous experts of Hawai'i, *kahuna*, were usually of this class.

Chiefs and chiefesses were granted special privileges forbidden to commoners, but their lives were at times difficult. Tales of *ali'i* cruelty abound, but most chiefs (and chiefesses) seem to have been generous, kind rulers sincerely concerned for the welfare of the people under their rule. Some Hawaiians today still trace their genealogy back to the *ali'i*, and even further back, to the *akua*.

Maka'ainana were the common people. They fished, farmed, trapped birds, made crafts, and raised families. Though they were common, the *ali'i* couldn't survive without them. The relationship between *ali'i* and *maka'ainana* was mutually beneficial.

Kauwa were similar to the "untouchables" of India. They were universally reviled slaves. Their shadows couldn't fall on anyone, not even a commoner. They were clearly distinguished from *maka'ainana* by the tattoos which were applied on their foreheads or at the corners of their eyes.

Kauwa were probably the descendants of groups who had been conquered in battle. They were often used in human sacrifice. They had no rights or privileges and were forced to live in small enclaves on specific pieces of land, like prisoners.

The idea of slaves and human sacrifice may seem abhorrent, but it's been just over 100 years since slaves were specially imported into this country, and there were still slaves on the mainland United States decades after they were officially freed in Hawai'i. And though human sacrifice might seem intolerable, most of the victims were criminals—and capital punishment is still in legal use in the United States.

Hawai'i: the land and its people. Examining a new culture can be challenging, for we naturally compare its values, religion, and practices with our own. Assuming that we accept our way of life as the ideal, it can be difficult to see the inherent value in any other.

Setting aside cultural bias allows us to truly learn, for we're not constantly judging new information according to our prejudices and expectations. An understanding of the people that created other cultures can be achieved only through unbiased thought and a willingness to learn.

Traditional Hawaiian spirituality may seem strange and alien, but it had at its core the goal of all religion: contact with the divine. Viewing these aspects of Hawaiian culture from a non-Western perspective can be quite rewarding.

Born of an antique Polynesian past, nurtured on incredibly beautiful islands by a proud people whose ancestors had risked everything to find new homes, ancient Hawaiian spirituality has much of value to teach us today. Among these lessons are reverence for the land, ecological fishing and farming techniques, sensible water use, the strength of the extended family unit, the correctness of religious diversity, and the concept of spiritual power that permeates everything in existence.

We do, indeed, have much to learn.

CHAPTER TWO

The Ways of the Deities

 "Amama ua noa!" The aged priest stands still as he finishes his prayer with these words ("Now the prayer has flown.") A dozen chiefs kneel before him. Nearby, a semi-circle of six-foot wooden images stares down, but it isn't to these that the *kahuna* turns.

Silence. The chiefs are immobile. The prayer priest's body tightens as he searches the skies and the earth for a sign that the *mana* of the prayer had been received by the deities.

He glances at the vegetables and fruits, at the piles of herbs and flowers placed on the altar. Wouldn't the sign come?

Wind suddenly sweeps through the open-air temple. Thunder crackles in the sky. Light, cool rain refreshes the earth. The *kahuna* smiles. Three such signs were proof that the gods had received his prayer, and that Kane would bless them with fine crops.

Hawaiians acknowledged a multiplicity of deities. Different and specific deities were worshipped in various places, on different islands, among certain families, and in all professions. This makes it impossible to discuss ancient Hawaiian spirituality from a Western perspective. They had no one major deity that was continuously and solely worshipped, and lacked a true hierarchy of divinities.

Ancient Polynesians arrived in the islands fully possessed of the spirituality of their former home. In time, new deities were discovered within the land, sea, and air. Some of the earlier-known deities had new adventures in Hawai'i. Tales of the births of gods and goddesses were often tangled over the centuries, and conflicting versions arose. The vast number of deities led Hawaiians to speak of *ka lehu o ke akua*—the 400,000 gods and goddesses.

Many non-Hawaiians have heard of only one Hawaiian deity, Pele, but there are countless others. Deities were connected with every part of life. Fishers prayed to fishing gods, canoe makers to their deity, athletes to those who ruled over their favorite sports. Additionally, specific places nurtured the worship of certain deities (such as Kilauea on

Lava bed near ocean, Big Island, Hawai'i

the Big Island, Pele's home), and many birds, sea creatures, and plants were not only associated with deities, they were deities themselves.

Hawaiians didn't believe in the deities; their religion wasn't that uncertain. Their relationships with their goddesses and gods were based on observation and experience, not mystical theory. Such relationships were born from emotional, mental, and sensory experiences interpreted and rationalized according to Hawaiian tradition.

In *The Polynesian Family System in Ka-u, Hawai'i*, E. S. Craighill Handy and Mary Kawena Pukui wrote of the Hawaiian *akua* as "persons." This is, perhaps, a clue to the realness of goddesses and gods to the old Hawaiians. It was this ability to perceive natural phenomena as sentient beings that was at the heart of traditional Hawaiian spirituality.

Hawaiians didn't merely recognize the deities' presences, they actively worshipped them. The *akua* were constantly acknowledged with ritual and prayer. Centuries before the missionaries arrived, Hawaiians were indeed religious.

Their religious practices were built upon personal experience with these forces. Hawaiians didn't decide that the volcano was represented by Pele, they discovered Pele's presence within it. Pele isn't represented by the volcano, and the volcano isn't a representation of Pele. They are one and the same—inseparable.

For an ancient Hawaiian to question the reality of the goddesses and gods would have been as absurd as to question the existence of the ocean, the rain, the thunder. The ocean exists. The rain exists. The thunder exists. Similarly, Kanaloa exists. Lono exists. Kane exists.

Ancient Hawaiians, then, worshipped deities who were quite real. Fish from the sea were the direct gift from the god Ku'ula. Water sprang up where Kane had thrust his digging stick into the ground. All ate from Lono's food gourd.

Hawaiian religion was firmly rooted in the Earth and in life itself. It was truly a religion of the people. Though esoteric secrets were certainly treasured by the elite *kahuna pule* (religious experts; priests), all had access to much religious wisdom, and everyone (priests, chiefs, men, women, and children) prayed.

All Deities Deserve Worship

In opposition to many other religions, traditional Hawaiian spirituality accepted that all *akua,* from every island and land, were genuine. Foreign gods were just as viable and deserving of worship and respect as were those that had been discovered by the Hawaiians.

The Reverend William Ellis, an English missionary who preached throughout Hawai'i in the 1820s, once met a priestess of Pele. After listening to his sermon, the priestess said to the people assembled there, "Powerful are the gods of Hawaii, and great is Pele, the goddess of Hawaii."

Rev. Ellis inquired whether she had heard and understood his sermon (which he had presented in Hawaiian). She replied that she had. Rev. Ellis then pointedly asked whether the woman thought that Jehovah was "good" and made his worshippers happy. The woman answered him:

> *He is your good god, and it is right that you should worship him; but Pele is my deity, and the great goddess of Hawai'i. Kilauea is the place of her abode. Ohiaokelani is one corner of her house. From the land beyond the sky, in former times, she came.*

After several such statements, Rev. Ellis tried once again to correct her, saying that Jehovah was the only god. She pointed out that this simply wasn't true (See Ellis, *Polynesian Researches: Hawaii,* pp. 309-310). This acceptance of a multiplicity of deities was central to traditional Hawaiian spirituality.

The Nature of the Deities

The gods and goddesses of Hawai'i possessed many human qualities. They loved, fought, succeeded, and failed. They planted, harvested, drank intoxicating beverages, surfed, and sailed. The greatest difference between humans and deities was *mana.* The *akua* possessed far more *mana* than did even the chiefly class.

The *akua* could be kind; or, if ignored (or their taboos broken), harsh. Each deity, to a certain extent, possessed these dual qualities; no one deity was thought of as the personification of evil. The ancient Hawaiians recognized no devil; they sensed that all people (including the deities) were whole and complete. Thus, even a sorcery *akua* could be invoked to restore life.

Some of these beings lived on the Earth. Others were spoken of as residing on other lands (islands), which humans were rarely allowed to visit. But the Hawaiians definitely viewed the *akua* as human-like. Goddesses and gods sledded down hills, surfed off favorite beaches, danced the *hula,* voyaged from island to island, flew kites, hunted and farmed, and interacted with humans—though usually with the *ali'i,* who were their closest relatives. Some *akua* fell in love with humans, and reports of the deaths of some of them are still extant.

This human nature of the *akua* isn't so mysterious. In his *Man, Gods and Nature,* Michael Kioni Dudley convincingly argues that all of the *akua* were once human beings who lived on this planet. (See page 70.) After their deaths, they were deified and worshipped. (See Chapter 3). This certainly explains why the *akua* are sometimes spoken of as living persons, and sometimes as divine entities. What we know today to be the deities were probably the earliest ancestral spirits worshipped, both in Hawai'i and throughout Polynesia.

Hawaiian genealogy was of great importance (at least to the chiefly class). Family trees usually reached back to *akua* ancestors, and this once again supports Dudley's concept.

The sacred stories of the *akua* (what others term "myths") form a rich and varied tapestry. (See Beckwith, etc.)

Homes of the Deities

There are many stories of the *akua* living in Hawai'i. There are also tales of their arrivals (which also supports the theory regarding their human nature). Most of the *akua,* however, also lived at various times on one of the 12 sacred islands under the jurisdiction of Kane. These islands may float on the sea, lie within its waters, or hang in the air shrouded by clouds. These "islands hidden by the gods" may sometimes be seen at sunrise or at sunset, on the distant horizon, bathed with reddish light.

The most famed of these "lost islands" (islands are the Polynesian equivalent of land) is Kane-huna-moku (hidden land of Kane), on which Kane (provider of fresh water, sunlight, and fertility) and Kanaloa (god of the ocean) reside. On this island the *akua* enjoy life without work or death, and tears are forbidden.

A second sacred land, Kuai-he-lani (supporting heaven), is often mentioned in sacred stories, as is yet a third, Nu'u-mea-lani (elevated hushed place in the heavens) which is famous as the land to which Haumea (the goddess presiding over childbirth) retires at various times before returning to earth in a new human form and producing new generations of offspring. Some authors state that Nu'u-mea-lani existed "above" Kuai-he-lani, and indeed that all of these lands existed one atop the other.

Comparisons of these lands to both heaven and the Garden of Eden should be avoided, as they seem to have been known in pre-Christian times. The concept of the gods residing in the sky is found throughout the world.

Such islands, then, were the temporary abodes of the *akua*. Humans could only occasionally visit them, usually by chance, and were so sacred that even when they were seen passing by, it was forbidden to point at them.

Prayer and Ritual

Hawaiians have always loved to pray, and prayers were the most common form of spiritual expression in old Hawai'i. An infinite variety of religious ritual was duly performed. Virtually every aspect of life—conception, birth, naming, nursing and weaning, marriage, house building, medicine, food production, sickness, and death, to name a few—was governed by specific deities.

Each occupation and handicraft, from weaving and carving to thievery and navigation, was watched over by a specific deity. Prayer to the appropriate deity was required before, during, and after the work.

This doesn't mean that Hawaiians were superstitious persons, for they possessed the scientific knowledge that allowed them to knot a net, build a house, fish, or plant bananas. Prayer was used to ensure that the knots were tight, that the house was built on stable ground, that the canoe wasn't swamped by waves on the open sea, and that the banana trees weren't touched by disease. Prayers were fervent requests that the respective deities watch over a project, guide its completion, and to bless and guard the finished product.

Formal prayers were fine, but anyone could and did pray at any time, for any reason. Such prayers were usually spontaneously composed and made in need. The nature of these prayers has been described as conversational, which indicates the directness of communication between human and *akua*.

Prayers performed within a temple by a *kahuna pule* (prayer priest) for the chiefs and common people might have been for fertility of the fields, success in battle, much-needed rain and other general blessings. Other types of *kahuna* (experts) said prayers for a variety of reasons on behalf of the people.

Such prayers had usually been composed in the distant past, expertly memorized and handed down to the next generation of priests. Not one word could be changed in such traditional prayers and many were recited in one breath.

These formal prayers—and, indeed, all prayers—were known to be powerful forces. Speaking these words, particularly when offering sacrifices at the altar, to the beat of a prayer drum, while the commoners stood in total silence, was more than a formalized rite. The prayer, and the words that composed it, possessed *mana*. The end of the prayer, in which the priest usually stated *amama ua noa* ("the prayer is now free or flown") signalled the moment at which the spiritual power generated by the prayer literally flew to the deity or deities. Prayer was much more than a simple recitation of words, it was the act of sending *mana* to the *akua*.

Words were of great importance to the ancient Hawaiians. They were not only a means of communicating thoughts and ideas, they were also a method of moving *mana*.

Deity Images

Early reports from missionaries and Christian-biased explorers were filled with references to the "hideous idols" that ancient Hawaiians made and used in their rites. Hawaiians did indeed make images of their *akua*. Such images *(ki'i)* greatly varied according to the deity to be represented. Most were made of wood (other materials include stone, feathers, bark cloth, and net made from local vines), and some didn't resemble humans.

Such figures were just that—figures, created by special experts or by anyone who was so inspired. Prayers and rituals were required before a *ki'i* was regarded as the home of a deity. Just as a prayer by a priest transforms a piece of bread during the Catholic rite of transubstantiation, so too did prayer transform statues into physical vehicles for the deities.

Hawaiians did perform acts of religious worship before such images of their deities; they were the foci of religious rites. But Hawaiians knew that the deities themselves surrounded them. Hawaiians didn't pray to pieces of wood; they prayed to the *mana* that was housed within these "artificial gods." In a sense, they acted as telephones to the deities who were there whether or not an image was present.

Offerings

Offering was a traditional and perhaps the preferred method of honoring the deities. This is logical: give to the gods and goddesses whom you most highly value. Sacrifices took many forms, depending on the deity being honored: bark cloth, fruits, flowers, ferns and other plants, vegetables, fish, chickens, eggs, black pigs, and (notoriously) humans.

Offerings at heiau *site, Kauaʻi*

The practice of human sacrifice has received much attention, but was far from the commonest offering.

The usual form of offering consisted of food. This was known as *mohai ʻai*. The Hawaiians understood that the deities ate only the essence of the offerings. Once the deities had their share, humans ate the remaining portion. Thus, though a black pig might be offered to Lono it also provided food for humans.

Only one *akua* demanded offerings of human sacrifice. This was Kukaʻilimoku, Kamehameha I's war god. No other deity was offered human sacrifices, and living human beings were never thrown into volcanoes. Additionally, women were never sacrificed.

The "Many Bodies" of the Deities

Most of the *akua* could assume many forms, or bodies, not all of which were human. These *kinolau* ("many" or "other bodies") included plants, fish, birds, rocks, and natural phenomena (such as clouds, lightning, or the wind). Thus, Pele was the volcano but could also appear as a flame, a young girl, a white dog, or an elderly woman at her will. These were among her many bodies. The agricultural deity Kane was seen in owls, sugarcane, and many other animals and plants.

Such a complex attitude toward the *akua* may at first be confusing, but it becomes easier to grasp with this simple concept: as I've already written, Pele is the volcano; the volcano is Pele. Similarly, Kane is thunder and sugarcane, and sugarcane and thunder are Kane. These aren't representations or personifications, they're simply different forms that the deities can take at will. The concept of *kinolau* is quite important in Hawaiian spirituality, as we'll see.

Why Are There Fewer Goddesses?

At this late date, it's difficult (if not impossible) to determine whether the seeming predominance of male deities in old Hawai'i is due to unbalanced reporting (by largely male investigators and explorers who were notorious for underplaying the importance of goddess worship), or whether goddesses simply didn't enjoy widespread worship in the past. Women, in general, certainly weren't treated as cattle in those days. Those of the *ali'i* class enjoyed many extra privileges. Some women even excelled in otherwise male-dominated occupations, such as the famous female *kaula* (prophets). (See Chapter 18.)

True, women were subjected to many taboos that didn't apply to men, but these were usually linked with specific male deities, or were directly related to menstruation. Hawaiians believed menstruation to be "defiling," but it's potentially true that men were simply frightened of the *mana* generated by a woman during menstruation.

At any rate, we know much more concerning the gods of old Hawai'i than we do of the goddesses. The notable exception, Pele, will be discussed in Chapter 4.

I preface the following chapters with these remarks so that I won't be accused of sexism by my presentation of the information. It seems likely that many aspects of women's spiritual lives of those times have been lost.

For example, one woman who is considered to be an expert on ancient Hawaiian culture boldly told me that "women didn't pray" in old Hawai'i. This statement was strenuously denied when I mentioned it to a *kahuna,* and most other experts agree that they did, indeed, pray.

Women can certainly pray to male deities, and men to goddesses. Still, goddess worship is naturally more common by women. In Hawai'i, as in many other societies, women lived enclosed in a small hut *(hale nea)* during menstruation each month. We simply can't know what secrets were shared at these times among female family members.

Women participated in certain "state" rituals, and there were women *kahuna,* but much has been lost. At least some information has been preserved.

The Four Great Gods

In Hawaiian spirituality, four deities were revered above all others (at least in formal group rituals). These were Ku, Kane, Lono, and Kanaloa.

Worship of these four *akua* was widespread, and temples built to honor Ku, Kane, and Lono are scattered over the islands. Each of these four deities (except, perhaps, Kanaloa) had his own priesthood and recognized forms of worship.

The worship of Ku, Kane, Lono, and Kanaloa was brought to the islands by the Polynesian settlers. All four are famous throughout Polynesia and, though they may be called by slightly different names, their sacred stories are similar, whether recited on New Zealand, Tahiti, Hawai'i, or elsewhere. (See Chapter 3 for more information.)

Belief in the Deities Today

Remnants of the old ways survive in Hawai'i, though many residents would be quick to contradict such an idea. Over a century of strict Christian training has converted many Hawaiians' viewpoint regarding their cultural heritage. Rituals and beliefs that were once treasured are now often publicly derided. Few cultural Hawaiians openly admit to having more than an intellectual curiosity in the religion of their ancestors.

This is understandable. Less than 30 years ago, Hawaiians were taught to be ashamed of their rich heritage. Interest in the ways of the grandparents or of any symbols of their heritage (such as *hula*) was deemed highly inappropriate. Only recently has a Hawaiian cultural renaissance allowed many Hawaiians to feel comfortable with their mother culture.

But the deities aren't dead, and neither is their worship. I once met a botanist who prayed to Ku for protection when she walked alone through the mountains. Some residents of the Volcano area of the Big Island openly admit to respecting Pele, and to leaving offerings to the goddess. Construction workers in Hawai'i often won't go to work until the site has first been blessed, by either a *kahuna* or a Christian priest, so that accidents won't occur. Old bones and offerings in burial caves are left undisturbed.

Secret rituals performed at night in isolated sacred sites continue to this day. Many serious *hula* students make pledges to Laka, the goddess of the *hula,* and temples on all the islands are always covered with offerings of fruit, flowers, and leaf-wrapped rocks by persons seeking blessings from the deities. No one can know how much worship continues, in various forms, within the privacy of the home.

The Hawaiian cultural renaissance that began in the 1970s and continues today has naturally led many Hawaiians to investigate their ancestors' spirituality. Even many who regularly attend church haven't yet forgotten the *akua.* This would, indeed, be impossible, for every rock, pool, lake, and mountain is steeped in sacred history, and the deities still walk the islands.

CHAPTER THREE

The Gods and Goddesses

The Major Gods

Kane

Kane is the provider of sunlight, fresh water, winds, and even the life-force itself: he ruled procreation and fertility. Said to have been born in antiquity of the union between Papa (the earth) and Wakea (the light; the sky), he came from Kahiki (the Hawaiians' ancestral home) with his constant companion, the god Kanaloa. The two were first sighted, in their human forms, off the coast of the island of Maui.

His worship was quite complex, for there were many forms of Kane. Some authorities list 30; others, 70. As Kanehekili, he was lightning; as Kanehoalani, ruler of the heavens. Kanehulikoa was his oceanic form. He was also Kane of the whirlwind, Kane of the rainbow, of the heavenly star, of the great wind, of the precipice—the list is extensive.

In human form, Kane is described as being dark complected with curly hair and thick lips. Kane's other *kinolau* include fresh water, some forms of coral, owls, sugar cane, certain forms of taro, *popolo* (a member of the nightshade family used medicinally), the albatross, and many other plants and animals. The color yellow is especially sacred to him.

Each family seems to have worshipped Kane in some form, usually as an *'aumakua* (deified ancestral spirit). Indeed, the family altar, at which daily prayer occurred, was known as Pohaku-o-Kane ("the stone of Kane"). This was generally a single, cone-shaped stone, from one to six feet high. (See Chapter 11.)

During worship, the stone was sprinkled with fresh water or coconut oil and covered with a piece of bark cloth. It was here that family members who had broken a taboo or who wished for some blessing prayed to Kane (and to other deities).

As giver of life in some sacred stories, Kane wasn't offered human sacrifice, for *ua kapu ke ola na Kane* ("life is sacred to Kane"). Among his favorite offerings were yellow bark cloth, pigs, and *'awa* (an intoxicating, non-alcoholic drink).

Though Kane did live for a time in Hawai'i, he is now said to reside on his cloud-shrouded island home Kane-huna-moku with his friend Kanaloa.

In Hawai'i today, great masses of clouds often float over the islands, pouring torrential rains on the windward (wet) sides. It is in these clouds that Kane can still be seen.

Ku

Like Kane, Ku had many forms. He was addressed as the sun in the morning. He was the god of fishing, war, forests, certain types of agriculture, rain, canoes, and some forms of sorcery. Though human sacrifices were offered to him, he was also invoked while gathering healing herbs.

Ku was often linked with the goddess Hina (see below). Together, they were invoked as great ancestral spirits. (Though virtually all Hawaiian *akua* are viewed as ancestral spirits, Ku was more widely invoked than most *'aumakua*.)

Ku is most famous today in his form of Kuka'ilimoku ("Ku the snatcher of land"). Worship of this war deity was brought to Hawai'i in the twelfth century by a Tahitian farmer-priest, Pa'ao, who had apparently left his homeland after a family fight that ended with Pa'ao killing his son and nephew.

As a deity of war, Kuka'ilimoku was enormously popular with the island's warring chiefs. Soon, the widespread worship of Kuka'ilimoku forever altered life in old Hawai'i.

Taboos were greatly increased, and breaking them became a capital offense. The various classes of society no longer mingled, and the temples were now closed to commoners, which had never before been the case. Pa'ao also introduced the practice of human sacrifice, a requirement in Kuka'ilimoku worship. The chief who would be king, Kamehameha I, was one of his most famous worshippers.

The aggressive, warring aspects of Kuka'ilimoku tend to overshadow the gentler side of Ku. Farmers invoked him when planting (as Ku-kulia and Ku-keolowalu); fishermen offered to him as Ku'ula.

One of the most charming sacred stories concerning Ku reveals his humane nature. Ku lived with a woman in Puna (on the island of Hawai'i) and fathered many children. Soon, however, a famine ravaged the land. Seeing that his children were starving, Ku went to his garden, said goodbye to his mate, and stood on his head.

He slowly sank into the ground until his body completely disappeared. His crestfallen mate watched the place for days, "watering it with her tears." Eventually, a plant sprouted. It grew into a great breadfruit tree that ended the famine and saved his family. That Ku could make such a selfless sacrifice for his family indicates that he wasn't solely a god of war who demanded bloody offerings. In his many bodies, Ku was just as complex as any human being.

Ku had many *kinolau*, including the hawk, a form of *'ohi'a lehua* (a plant related to the bottlebrush), the coconut, breadfruit, the *ki* plant, the eel, and the *loli* (sea cucumber). The color red was especially sacred to him.

Worship of Ku produced the most spectacular and elaborate *heiau* (temples). When a chief was about to wage war against another chief, he often built a new *heiau* to Ku. Kamehameha built the largest, best preserved, and most recent *luakini heiau* (human sacrificial temple) in the islands: Pu'ukohola on the Big Island, which was recently the site of a celebration marking the 200th anniversary of its construction.

Ku is, indeed, a god of contrasts. He can still be seen every morning as the sun rising from ocean, mountain, or plain; in the groves of coconut trees; in the dense undergrowth of the forests; in the hawks that hypnotically glide over the islands.

Lono

Lono is the god of peace, sports, fertility, and agriculture. He's seen in the clouds, wind, rain, thunder, storms, whirlwinds, waterspouts, gushing springs, and the sounds of wind and rain. Most importantly, Lono was the provider of food.

His worship was widespread. Each family's men's eating house contained a symbol of Lono. This was a food gourd covered with netting or wickerwork and attached to a notched stick (known as *pule ipu;* literally, "prayer gourd"). In this gourd were placed various kinds of food, including fish and the rootstock *'awa.* At morning and evening the head of the household removed the gourd from the netting, laid it at the door, and prayed. Once the prayers were finished, he ate the food from the gourd and sucked or prepared and drank the *'awa.*

In his human form, Lono was a light-skinned man. Among his many bodies was that of a pig or a man-pig. In this form, Lono was known as Kamapua'a, who was famous for his tempestuous relationship with Pele. Most of his other *kinolau* were in some way (usually through resemblance) related to pigs.

He could also swim between the islands as the fish *humu-humu-nuku-nuku-apua'a.* He was seen as the *'aholehole* and other kinds of fish, in the *kukui* tree, and in a variety of the taro.

Temples built for Lono were the centers of prayers for rain, abundant crops, and healing. Offerings to Lono included pigs, certain types of coconuts, and all manner of fruits and vegetables, but never human beings. Those who were too poor to offer a pig in sacrifice to Lono could substitute one of his fish.

As patron of agriculture, Lono ensured that his people weren't hungry. Even when drought swept the islands, as infrequently happened, famine foods could be gathered from the forests. Lono guarded his children.

Lono presided over the annual *makahiki* celebrations, which were held on every island for four consecutive months, usually from October or November through February or March. This was a time of ritual, sports competitions, offerings to the chiefs, divination of the fruitfulness of the coming year, and much feasting and *hula*.

During the *makahiki* war was forbidden, people did little work and enjoyed themselves. The taboos were lessened and the war temples of Ku were closed (since warfare wasn't permitted during this period). As many as 5,000 people, dressed in their finest clothing and ornaments, gathered to participate.

The dating of the *makahiki* was determined by the first appearance of the Pleiades above the horizon at dusk, which yearly occurs from late October to early November. At this time Lono traditionally arrived from Kahiki (the traditional Hawaiian term for the ancestral homeland). He landed at Kealakekua in the Kona district of the Big Island where Captain James Cook would eventually have a deadly confrontation after being mistaken for the god in human form.

An image of Lono was created for the *makahiki*, which consisted of a tall upright wooden pole, at the top of which was a crosspiece. A carved figure surmounted the pole (some say it was a human head; others, a bird), and from the crossbar hung sheets of white bark cloth and *lei* of fern and feathers. This portable symbol of the deity (termed *Lonomakua;* "Father Lono") was carried throughout the island while offerings (such as pigs, taro, sweet potatoes, feathers, mats, and bark cloth) were collected from all.

The sports competitions over which Lono presided during the *makahiki* included Hawaiian forms of bowling, boxing, wrestling, sledding, running, and many other activities. These competitions usually occurred in November.

Sports were viewed as spiritual activities, and each sport was presided over by a specific deity. Those participants with the most *mana* usually won. (The *makahiki* has recently been revived on O'ahu, with feasting, *hula,* athletic competitions, and other activities taking place on an annual basis.)

Lono is still to be seen in Hawai'i in the fruitfulness of the fields.

Kanaloa

Little is known of Kanaloa today. In fact, he's best known as a companion of Kane. Their names were often linked in chants, even when Ku and Lono weren't specifically and immediately mentioned.

One story states that Kanaloa and Kane (who are separated only with difficulty) came together from the Hawaiian's ancestral homeland (Kahiki). They were banana cultivators, avid drinkers of 'awa, and inveterate water-finders, especially in dry areas of the islands. They travelled extensively throughout the islands, sometimes settling down for a time at certain spots, such as the beautifully wild Waipio Valley on the Big Island.

Both were associated with fish and with fish ponds (artificially dammed lakes used to raise fish for food). Certain fish (such as the delicious 'ama'ama, mullet) are said to have followed Kanaloa and Kane to Hawai'i from Kahiki. Described as being tall and fair, in common with other *akua,* Kanaloa is best known as a god of the sea. Kanaloa was invoked for smooth sailing and for protection while at sea. The tides were created as he breathed in and out.

Included among his many bodies was the octopus, which played a role in healing ceremonies. (The octopus was frequently known as squid in Hawai'i.) During the ceremony, the patient was put to bed. The *kahuna* said a prayer over the patient, entreating Kanaloa in his squid guise to heal the patient.

Very early the next morning, accompanied by another chant in which Kanaloa is once again identified with the squid "that lies flat," the healing *kahuna* caught an octopus while it lay with its legs stretched out on the sand in the ocean. He then, presumably, returned and performed the healing. (The symbolism of the slippery squid and the disease "slipping" from the patient is obvious.)

Among Kanaloa's other "bodies" were the banana and a plant (*ala'alapuloa*) used in healing. He was worshipped with offerings of *'awa*, whitefish (*'aholehole*), pigs, and other food items.

Sources of fresh water throughout the islands were ascribed to the exertions of Kane and Kanaloa with their *o'o* (digging sticks).

A few sacred stories have been interpreted to indicate that Kanaloa was connected with the Hawaiian underworld. Such associations later led Christian missionaries to falsely link this gentle deity with the devil—an entirely unjustified conclusion.

Some sources state that Kanaloa wasn't recognized as a deity on Kaua'i. He was perhaps less well-known than the other major gods, but he lives still in the surging waters that surround Hawai'i and bless it with fruitfulness.

The Major Goddesses

This is a personal selection, but the above four entries are so overwhelmingly male that I felt that equal time was appropriate. Once again, a shortage of information concerning the goddesses plagues all Hawaiian researchers.

We'll meet the most famous of Hawaiian goddesses, Pele, in the following chapter.

Haumea

Haumea is the Earth-mother who presided over childbirth. She's a complex figure. Some chants sing that she is also Papa, the primordial mate of Wakea, who lived as a mortal woman and became an important ancestor of the Hawaiian people. Some say that she was the mother of Pele. Still others state that Haumea was a woman who was born with Kane and Kanaloa. As this woman, La'ila'i, she was regarded as the creatrix of the Hawaiian people (and as the first woman ever created, with Ki'i, the first man).

In most of her sacred stories one fact is clear: Haumea gave birth to many, many children. This is responsible for her powers over childbirth. Apparently none of her children were born in the normal manner: they sprang from different parts of her body. Despite this somewhat unusual ability Haumea acted as divine midwife to many human mothers.

One sacred story says that she arrived with her brothers Kane and Kanaloa in South Kona on the Big Island. Two fishermen who happened to notice their arrival worshipped them. Haumea's relationship with one of these fishermen produced a daughter who was born from her head.

Her skill at childbirth is recounted in many stories. On one occasion she intervened when childbirth was unduly delayed. Hearing the mother's wails and seeing that the attending *kahuna* were preparing for a caesarean section, she appeared and said that cutting the woman wouldn't be necessary if she ate a remedy prepared from a certain tree. The pregnant woman's attendants carried out her instructions. Haumea pressed against the woman's thighs and the child was born without incident.

At another time, Haumea agreed to act as midwife for a chiefess. Haumea's prayers and incantations allowed the chiefess to painlessly give birth. She was rewarded with a magic tree that possessed two blossoms, one of which produced musical notes. Eventually, through no fault of her own, this tree was carved into *ki'i* (sacred images). The tree may have been a form of bamboo, from which nose flutes were made.

Her control over fertility extended also to that of the plants in forest wildernesses.

Haumea's traditional home, Nu'umealani, was one of the sacred islands of the *akua*. On O'ahu, it was chanted that she had the power to assume many human forms, from young to old, through the use of a magical "fish-drawing branch."

Her human form is said to have lived on O'ahu, on the northern side of the Kahili Valley, but she seemed to frequently travel back and forth from here to two homes of the deities: Nu'umealani and Kuai-helani.

One variety of breadfruit *(ulu)* was sacred to her. This was the low-lying form that grew like a bush (called *'uluhua i ka hapapa*). Haumea is referred to as a mysterious *akua,* but she still presides over childbirth in Hawai'i.

Hina

Hina was one of the great ancestral goddesses of old Hawai'i. She was intimately linked with the moon. When associated with Ku, prayers to her were directed to the west (as those to Ku were to the east). Some persons, however, prayed to Hina to the east as Hinakua (progenitor of those who have yet to be born), and toward the west as Hinaalo (mother of those humans who have already been born). She was recognized as the mother of the Hawaiian people, and also ruled the procreative powers of women.

Hina was sometimes thought of as presiding over all female *akua.* She had many forms, one of which is said to have been the mother of the famous demi-deity Maui. She's also intimately connected with the Hawaiian island Moloka'i.

Some of her many forms include Hina'opuhalako'a, goddess of corals and other spiny creatures of the sea. This form of Hina could appear as both a coral reef and as a woman. Other oceanic forms of Hina include Hina-lau-limu-kala (Hina of the leaves of the *limu kala* seaweed), patroness of *kahuna* who used medicines from the sea, and Hinapukai'a, the wife of Ku'ula (the fishing god form of Ku). As Hina-i-kapa'i-kua she beat bark to make cloth, and she was also seen in the forests of *'ohi'a lehua* that grow on the Big Island.

Perhaps her most famous form, however, involved her relationship with the moon. She was frequently known as Hina-i-ka-malama, ("Hina in the moon"), and her sacred story is still told: Hina worked day after day at the laborious process of creating *kapa* (bark cloth). Finally, tiring of this ceaseless labor, she packed her *ipu* (gourd) and travelled by the "rainbow path" up to the sun. This proved far too hot to be her new home, so she climbed to the moon, although her

Waimea Canyon, Kaua'i

husband tried to force her to stay on the Earth. Today, when the full moon shines, Hina can still be seen on the moon.

From the ocean to the forests, even to the moon, Hina was an important deity in old Hawai'i. Her direct spiritual links with Ku (some families recognized both as their ancestors) prove the prominence of her worship in ancient Hawai'i. Even today, *kahuna* may yet address her and Ku as they collect medicinal herbs, and she still shines on tropic nights on the face of the moon.

Laka

The name Laka is used to refer to three persons: a god worshipped by canoe carvers, a young (male) navigator famous for his canoe (which had been built by the *menehune*—see Chapter 15), and the goddess of *hula* and of forest plants. It this final Laka that will be here discussed.

The worship of Laka in old Hawai'i took one of the most poetic forms. Her altars were temporary structures, built of entwined branches and decorated with forest ferns, flowers, and other plants. As the altar was being built, the *kumu hula* (hula teacher) chanted songs of praise to Laka. The many plants used to decorate and scent her altar were among her *kinolau*. The goddess was represented on her altar by a block of *lama* (a local type of ebony) wood covered with a piece of yellow *kapa* (yellow and red were colors of divinity among the *akua*, and royalty among the *ali'i*—see Chapter 12). As with many other deities, she was offered bowls of *'awa* each day.

Though students and practitioners of the divine art of *hula* worshipped many other deities, Laka was the patron (and creatrix) of the dance, and so it was to her that they directed much of their honor. She was also sometimes invoked as a goddess of love.

Some chants refer to Laka as sister to Lono, god of agriculture and weather. She is said to have been the daughter of Kapo (a goddess of sorcery and Pele's sister) who, in turn, was a daughter of the mysterious goddess Haumea.

Some traditional *hula* schools still dedicate their dancers to Laka, and most dancers make plans to visit the famous temple dedicated to Laka on Kaua'i (at Ke'e Beach) at least once during their lifetimes.

Some of the old chants are still in use. *Hula* competitions are as popular in Hawai'i as football playoffs are on the mainland. *Hula*, once banned and nearly driven out of existence by ignorant outsiders, then restored in popularity by King Kalakaua, has become an outward symbol of the rich Hawaiian heritage.

Laka lives on today in the practice of *hula*.

Ka'ahupahau

Ka'ahupahau was worshipped in a limited area, but she remains famous to this day due to this location. She lived in a cave with her son (or brother) near the entrance to Pearl Harbor. Ka'ahupahau was widely honored because she guarded the waters off O'ahu from man-eating sharks. The beautiful orange blossoms of the *'ilima* were sacred to her.

What makes her so unusual is that she was born of human parents. She was described as a girl with light-colored hair who was transformed into a shark. Her brother/son also experienced this transformation.

Unlike some other sharks, however, Ka'ahupahau and her son were kind creatures. Persons who lived in Ewa on O'ahu fed and cared for these two sharks, and in return they protected the people when they swam and were thus subject to shark attacks. Her caretakers even kept her back clean of barnacles by scraping them off at regular intervals.

Acknowledgement of her existence has continued to the present century. A new dry dock was built in Pearl Harbor in about 1914 and immediately collapsed. It was widely stated that Ka'ahupahau was still present in Pearl Harbor. Resenting this intrusion into her realm, she destroyed it.

In old Hawai'i, sharks were one of many 'aumakua, family spirits worshipped by humans as forms of divine ancestors. This wasn't symbolic: many Hawaiians accepted the fact that they were directly related to sharks. Ka'ahupahau was most certainly first an 'aumakua who eventually was worshipped even by those who weren't her descendants. Some stories say that she was killed during the famous shark war, or that she ate a chiefess who dared to enter Ka'ahupahau's waters wearing an 'ilima lei. Still, "she of the smiting tail" swims to this day in the very changed waters of Pearl Harbor.

Hi'iaka

Beloved younger sister of Pele, Hi'iaka was born to her mother, Haumea, in the form of an egg. Pele, entrusted to guard the egg by her mother, kept it under (or between) her breasts. This is why she is sometimes known as Hi'iaka-i-ka-poli-o-Pele ("Hi'iaka in the bosom of Pele"). In due time Hi'iaka was "born."

She is an expert hula dancer, a healer, and guardian, seen in both the sky (as Hi'iaka-i-ka-maka-o-ka'opua: "Hi'iaka in the face of the rain clouds") and in fresh water (Hi'iakaikawaiola: "Hi'iaka in the waters of life"). She warned fishermen of dangerous storms at sea by appearing in the form of a small red rainbow. Hi'iaka gained the powers of a goddess from her sister, Pele. These powers allowed her to restore the dead to life, fend off dangerous creatures, have psychic visions, and to be conversant in all forms of magic. She was also a healer invoked by *kahuna la'au lapa'au* (herbal doctors).

She was associated with many plants, including the scarlet pompom flowers of the *'ohi'a lehua*. A type of fern was also sacred to her, as was the *hala*, whose orange fruits are often found floating on the sea.

Hi'iaka was worshipped by her human descendants as a family ancestral deity as well as a goddess, especially by dancers.

Hi'iaka is most famous today for falling in love with one of Pele's beloved young chiefs, and for her dangerous journeys, battles with monsters, and for bearing the wrath of her volcanic sister.

Other Deities

There were many other *akua* honored in old Hawai'i. Most of them have almost slipped into obscurity, but some knowledge of their divine natures has remained. Those *akua* worshipped in small areas are the least well-remembered. Here are some brief entries; no such listing can be considered to be complete. Some of these "people" are *akua* and others are *'aumakua,* but all were worshipped.

'Ai'Ai: An *akua* of fishermen; son of Ku'ula. He found good fishing areas and built fishing shrines along the coasts.

'Aila'au: The ancient god of fire (his name means "wood eater"). He was worshipped in Hawai'i before the coming of Pele and her family. His worship was quickly consumed by that dedicated to Pele. He was responsible for the destructive fires that destroyed the beautiful forests of the Pun district of Hawai'i. He once lived in Kiluaea Iki (a small pit crater), but later moved into what would become Pele's home. However, when Pele finally reached the Big Island and visited 'Aila'au's home, he was nowhere to be found. Frightened by her great *mana*, he fled and was never seen again.

Ha'inakolo: Goddess of *kapa* makers and of bird catchers.

Koolau Mountains, Oahu

Hi'iaka-i-ka-maka-o-ka-'opua: Hi'iaka in the face of the rain clouds.

Hi'iaka-i-ka-wai-ola: The healing aspect of Hi'iaka.

Hi'iaka-makole-wawahi-wa'a: An aspect of Hi'iaka who warned fishermen at sea of dangerous winds and waves by appearing as a short red rainbow.

Hi'iaka-noho-lani: Hi'iaka, dweller in the sky. An aspect of Hi'iaka seen in the heavens.

Hinaalo: Mother of the Hawaiian people, addressed in prayer to the west.

Hina'ea: Goddess of the sunrise and sunset, this Hina had the ability to cure the common childhood disease of *'ea* (thrush). She also made fine bark cloth.

Hinahele: A goddess of fishermen and of women who was worshipped at small shrines by the sea. The fish *'ohua* belong to her.

Hina-i-ka-malama: Hina in the moon.

Hina-lau-limu-kala: Patron of *kahuna* who used medicines gathered from the sea. Her name means "Hina of the leaves of the (seaweed) *limu-kala*."

Hina-kua: Mother of those who have not yet been born. She was addressed in prayer to the east.

Hina-olu-'ohia: Hina of the growing *'ohia* tree.

Hina'opuhala-ko'a: A goddess of coral and spiny sea creatures. The coral reefs were sacred to her. A form of Hina.

Hina-pu-kai-'a: Mate of Ku'ula and a goddess of the fishermen.

Hokeo: An *akua* who helped Lono in bringing winds to Hawai'i. One of his *kinolau* was a gourd. (Hokeo was also type of gourd used to store food, clothing, and other materials.)

Ka-'alae-nui-a-hina: A great *'alae* bird (mudhen) of Hina. She possessed the secret of fire-making long before the demi-deity Maui stole it from her and shared the secret with humans. Ka-'alae-nui-a-hina was also invoked as a goddess of sorcery.

Kaiona: A goddess worshipped in a relatively small area on the island of O'ahu, she assisted those who became lost in the forest by sending a small bird guide, who led confused travellers to trails.

Kamapua'a: An aspect of Lono. He usually appeared as a hog or as a hog-man, but could take numerous other forms, including many plants, fish, and a handsome young man. He fell in love with Pele.

Kalaipahoa: The poison god, worshipped in the form of trees or of images made from these trees, into which sorcery *akua* had entered.

Kamohoali'i: One of Pele's shark brothers, who accompanied her on the journey from Kahiki to Hawai'i. Worshipped as an *'aumakua* and was greatly loved and respected. In human form, he appeared naked— a sign of divinity.

Kane-hekili: God of thunder; his body was thunder itself. Seen in dreams by his followers as a man. One side of his body is black, the other white.

Kane-hohoio: God of the threshold.

Kanepoha(ku)ka'a: "Rolling stone of Kane." God of stones to whom warriors prayed before battle.

Kapo: A goddess with two distinct sides to her personality. She was both a gentle patroness (sometimes identified with Laka) of *hula,* but was also invoked during works of destructive magic. Kapo was the sister of Pele and daughter of Haumea. After she migrated to Hawai'i, Kapo established a *hula halau* (dance school) on each of the islands, and was often invoked with Laka in chants. As Kapo-'ula-kina'u ("Kapo red-spotted") she was invoked to send evil power back to he or she who had sent it. Among her *kinolau* (many bodies) were the *hala pepe* plant, used on the *hula* altars, and the tree *'ohe* (exact identification of this tree hasn't yet been determined). She is said to have been most widely worshipped (by sorcerers, that is) on Maui.

Hawiian fisherman

Kapu-alakai: Healing goddess worshipped by women and by medicinal practitioners.

Kiha-wahine: A *mo'o 'aumakua* originally worshipped on Maui and Hawai'i. Her worship was spread throughout Hawai'i by Kamehameha I.

Ku-hai-moana: Shark god, brother of Pele and husband of the shark goddess Ka'ahu-pahau. (Not an aspect of Ku.)

Ku-huluhulu-manu: God of bird catchers and worshipped by all who performed feather work.

Ku-ka-'il-imoku: "Snatcher of land;" he is a war god. His worship, which required human sacrifice, is said to have begun in Hawai'i in the twelfth century. One of Kamehameha I's deities. An aspect of Ku worshipped by chiefs.

Kuka'o'o: A god of the farmers, and especially of the digging stick, *'o'o.* An aspect of Ku.

Ku-pulupulu: God of the forest and also of canoe makers. An aspect of Ku.

Ku'ula: One of the gods of the fishermen. An aspect of Ku.

Kuwahailo: A sorcery god, aspect of Ku. (The name means "Ku of the maggot-dripping mouth.")

La'ama'oma'o: A goddess who caused winds and storms to arise. She gave her son, Paka'a, an *'umeke* (covered wooden bowl) which contained the bones of La'ama'oma'o's grandmother. Through the use of this, and by chanting the names of the winds, he controlled them for navigational and other purposes.

La'ahana: The goddess of bark cloth makers. Daughter of Maikoha, god of *kapa* makers.

Laka: Goddess of the *hula.*

Lea: A goddess of canoe makers, who, in her *kinolau* as a bird *('ele-naio),* tested trees selected to be formed into canoes for internal soundness before they were cut and worked. Women (who didn't make canoes) also worshipped her.

Lilinoe: A goddess of mists. She is the younger sister of Poliahu, the Hawaiian snow goddess. Said to reside in Haleakala on Maui. Some sacred stories say that she lived with the goddess Poliahu on Mauna Kea on the island of Hawai'i.

Limaloa: On Kaua'i, a god of mirages. He guarded the sea.

Lono: God of peace, rain, agriculture, and fertility. Bringer of fertility to the Earth. Worshipped during the Makahiki festival. Among his *kinolau* are clouds, rain, thunder, lightning, earthquakes, waterspouts, waves, the sweet potato, the gourd, and the pig.

Maikoha: The god of bark cloth makers, father of La'ahana. From his grave was said to have grown the first *wauke* tree (source of the finest bark cloth).

Ma'iola: A god of healing, life, and health. He apparently was never physically represented in any form, but was worshipped by healing *kahuna*. He could occupy specific types of trees, the wood of which would counteract sorcery performed with the wood of other trees.

Makani-ke-oe: A god of winds, invoked during *hana aloha* (love magic).

Makua'aihue: A god worshipped by thieves.

Maui: A *kupua* (half-human, half-divine) born of the union of Hina and a human man (whose name varies). Maui is known as a trickster, but with the assistance of his great *mana* performed many miraculous deeds that assisted humans: he stole the secret of fire-making from the famous mudhens of Waianae on O'ahu and shared it with humans; he snared the sun so that it would move more slowly over the earth, enabling humans to do more work; and as a child he fished up the islands of Hawai'i with his magic hook, called Manai-a-ka-lani. Often associated with the island which shares his name, Maui was also known on all the Hawaiian islands, and throughout Polynesia.

Milu: God of the underworld. Little pre-Christian information concerning him is available, since missionaries linked him with Satan, resulting in tangled, false descriptions of this *akua*.

Na-maka-o-ka-ha'i: Sister of Pele; the ocean goddess who pursued Pele from Kahiki to Hawai'i, and there finally destroyed her.

Niuloahiki: God of the coconut tree. He could assume three forms: that of a coconut tree, an eel, or a man.

Niolopua: The Hawaiian god of sleep. His name is translated as "handsome," and he was invoked to end insomnia.

Nu'akea: She was invoked to bring milk to the breasts of nursing mothers.

'Opelu-nui-kau-ha'alilo: A deity of thieves; also a god of medicinal plants.

Papa: A primordial creatrix goddess, divine ancestress of the Hawaiian people. She resided with Wakea (whom, it is sometimes said, was human, not an *akua*). It is said that Papa gave birth to an *ipu* (gourd). Wakea threw the *ipu*'s cover up, where it became the sky. From the meat inside the gourd Wakea made the sun, the seeds became the stars, the white lining was transformed into the moon, the white meat Wakea made into clouds. He poured the juice onto the clouds to produce rain, and from the bowl of the gourd itself he created the land and the sea. One other child of Papa was born deformed, without arms or legs. He was buried at midnight; the next morning the stalk and leaves of the *kalo* (Tahitian *taro*) plant appeared. This is why *poi*, which is made from *kalo*, is sacred: the plant which furnishes this food sprang from the body of a son of Papa. In other sacred stories she individually gave birth to each of the Hawaiian islands.

Pele: Daughter of Haumea; among her many bodies are volcano, flame, and human forms. She lives at Halema'uma'u, Island of Hawai'i.

Poliahu: She is the snow goddess of the snow-covered mountain Mauna Kea, on the Big Island of Hawai'i. Sister of Lilinoe. She wears a white mantle (of snow) and is physically cold. In one sacred story, Hina-i-ka-malama (a form of Hina) struggles with Poliahu for a monogamous relationship with a handsome young chief, who has slept with them both. Poliahu is described as being beautiful. She sometimes resides at Haleakala on Maui (which occasionally receives snow).

Uli: The great goddess of sorcery who was invoked by the *kahuna 'ana'ana* (priests who prayed others to death). Though feared, she was also invoked to restore life to the dead and to bring health to all.

Wakea: With Papa, the progenitor of humans. A primordial god.

CHAPTER FOUR

Pele

Pele is perhaps the most famous of the Hawaiian *akua* and *'aumakua*. Her sacred stories are many. The continuing ritual recognition of Pele proves that traditional Hawaiian spirituality hasn't yet become extinct, in spite of more than 170 years of Christian influence.

Pele's Family

Like any other woman, Pele has a family. She was born to Haumea, the mysterious goddess, and Kane-hoa-lani. Among her sisters are Hi'iaka and Na-maka-o-ka-ha'i, a goddess of the sea. Her brothers Ka-mo'o-ali'i and Kane-'apua had shark bodies, and it was the first of these brothers who guided her canoe on its trip from Kahiki to Hawai'i. Ka-mo'o-ali'i was the eldest of her brothers, and Pele greatly loved him.

She has many more siblings: Kuku'ena-i-ke-ahi-ho'omau-honua is a younger sister who made Pele's *'awa* and who created *lei*. Another sister, Kapo-'ula-kina-u, was a form of Kapo, the goddess invoked in sorcery. She arrived in Hawai'i before Pele. Pele also has brothers associated with volcanic explosions.

Why did Pele come to Hawai'i? Chants say that she had no choice; she was forced from her home by the wicked doings of her sister Na-maka-o-ka-ha'i, a goddess with power over the seas.

Pele Comes to Hawai'i

There was trouble in Pele's family in Kahiki (Tahiti). Her sister, Na-maka-o-ka-ha'i, made life unbearable for her and her volcanic brothers. A being of volcanic activity and fires, Pele was constantly tortured by her sister, who sent the waters of the ocean rolling over her home to snuff out her flames. Finally, she received permission from her father to leave Kahiki. Pele carved a canoe. Those relatives who agreed to travel with her boarded the canoe. Also along were 40,000 deities, including Ku and Lono. Guided by her shark-bodied brother, the party sailed across the Pacific, barely surviving the continuous attacks upon their *wa'a* (canoe) by Na-maka-o-ka-ha'i.

Eventually, they landed on the small island Ni'ihau (now closed to outside visitors). Pele immediately set about finding a new home for her extended volcanic family. Using her magic digging stick she tried to create a home on the island, but her sister Na-maka-o-ka-ha'i sent water into it to quench its flames.

Undaunted, Pele moved on to Kaua'i, where she dug even deeper holes. Once again, ground water (a "gift" from her sea sister) destroyed them in the bursts of steam that were generated when the water hit Pele's fires. (Two of these holes can still be seen as caves near Ke'e beach on Kaua'i.) Her struggle with her sister forced her to leave Kaua'i.

Frustrated, Pele and her party travelled on to O'ahu. There she dug potential homes at Koko, Leahi (Diamond Head), Pu'uowaina (Punchbowl), Salt Lake, Moanalua, and elsewhere, but everywhere her sister's waters boiled up from the earth and destroyed her homes.

And so she voyaged to Maui where, in the great crater Haleakala, her sister again thwarted her search. On each island she had battled with her sister the sea goddess, but had always managed to survive.

However, some legends state that Ha-maka-o-ka-ha'i finally succeeded in killing Pele on Maui, and huge masses of broken lava there are still pointed out as Ka Iwi o Pele (Pele's bones).

Her sister was sure that she'd finally beaten Pele, but Ha-maka-o-ka-ha'i's jubilation was short. Pele's spirit travelled on to the island of Hawai'i and there, at Kilauea, dug an incredibly deep fire pit for her home. This home, situated many miles from the coast, was safely out of her sister's reach, and Pele and the volcanic members of her family moved in.

Pele the Goddess

Pele seems to have been a wholly Hawaiian deity, unlike many other *akua* who are known throughout Polynesia. She had two major types of *kinolau* (other bodies, besides the volcano): human and flame. As a human, she could appear as any age, but often took the form of a young chiefess of "surpassing beauty" when she wished to walk with humans. She could also appear as an elderly woman. She was an expert sledder and surfer. (This ability to assume different *kinolau*, in part, defines her divinity.) Pele could also appear as a little white dog which can still be seen today. In the past, before this period of continuous volcanic eruptions (which began in 1983), sighting the dog was viewed as an omen that the volcano was about to erupt.

Pele was greatly loved and honored as a *kupuna* (ancestress), and many families that lived on the island of Hawai'i could, through genealogical chants, trace their lineage back to Pele. This is still true today among some families.

In the distant past, she seems to have been recognized exclusively as an 'aumakua (family ancestor spirit). Eventually, though, her worship grew so widespread (and her *mana* so powerful) that her fame spread, and even those outside of her family made offerings to her. To this day, she is a goddess to non-related persons and an 'aumakua to relations.

Pele and her family live deep inside Kilauea. When she's calm, the fertile land of Hawai'i is also calm. But when Pele becomes angry, the

Kalapana lava site, Big Island, Hawai'i

earth shakes and becomes hot; the ground splits open and another eruption begins.

Pele is often thought of as a cruel goddess. This is untrue. Yes, she has a temper, and possesses the power to vent her anger in a spectacular fashion, but her worshippers accept this as part of her nature (much as a family might accept the vocal outbursts of a child or parent).

That Pele has a dark side has never been argued. This is true of all the Hawaiian deities. Any of the *akua,* if offended by broken *kapu* or a lack of offerings to them, could send misfortunes to humans.

Today, however, we know Pele as a true mother goddess who creates new land with every violent outpouring of lava into the sea. She is also at work some miles off the coast of the island of Hawai'i, where the seamount Loihi steadily and slowly grows from the ocean floor. Eventually, it will be the newest Hawaiian island.

This dual nature (destruction and creation) is certainly part of Pele's appeal. She is known today around the world, when many of the other deities are only recognized in Hawai'i itself. The reasons for this fact are quite clear: Pele is still visibly present on Hawai'i.

Worship of Pele

As previously stated, she was probably first worshipped as an *'aumakua*. Her human family members made offerings of *'awa,* pigs, and *ohelo* berries. These families usually lived on the Big Island of Hawai'i. Curiously, no images of Pele have ever been found or identified.

Priests and priestesses of Pele also existed. Little is known about their rites and duties. It is said that they worshipped her in *heiau* (temples) built quite close to areas of active vulcanism, particularly near lava flows or Halema'uma'u (the fire pit of Kilauea). Apparently, these small temples have all been covered with lava.

These special persons were known as *kaula Pele* (Pele's prophets). They acted as her earthly representatives. In any case, the *kaula Pele* officiated at rituals dedicated to Pele. Since a *kaula* is a prophet, this *kahuna* could also look into the future, or be possessed *(noho)* by the goddess so that she could speak with her people.

The *kaula Pele* were instructed from youth, and were treated with respect. With training they would eventually gain expert skills in some form of priest-craft. They became *kahuna.*

The most sacred of rituals dedicated to Pele was one of *kaku'ai* (transformation) in which a deceased family member was ritually transfigured into a spirit that dwelled with Pele. Such rituals were quite common in old Hawai'i, and weren't limited to Pele worship.

It was a long rite. The family members brought the body of the deceased, or some part of it (hair, nail clippings, bones), and offerings (*'awa,* a pig, a garment), as well as a gifts to the priests who were to perform the ceremony. The grieving family members, who might have numbered as many as 40, went with the *kaula Pele* to Halema'uma'u at Kilauea.

The pig was ritually killed as an offering of hope that the deceased, whose spirit was a newcomer to Pele's home, would be admitted to her realm. Pouring rain and thunder were signs that the offering had been accepted, and that the deceased would be welcomed.

The next morning, the pig that had been killed was roasted (but not eaten), and the party feasted. The *kaula Pele* then took the body of the dead one to the "very center of the fires" of the volcano. The genealogy of the deceased was chanted to prove her or his ancestral relationships with Pele. The pig and other offerings were thrown into the lava with prayer. The deceased's body followed it. The spirit of the dead had, if everything had gone correctly, become one with Pele and was reunited with his or her ancestors.

Pele's Hair

Pele has associations with hair. Her priests (some say that, in the earliest days, she had no priestesses) were sacred, and enjoyed many privileges. However, they weren't allowed to cut their hair except at the crater itself. It was there that they trimmed their hair and then threw the cuttings into the fire-pit, Pele's home.

Women with brown hair were thought to be especially sacred to Pele, although such a woman could also actually be the goddess. Even boys born with this color hair (perhaps it was a specific shade) were viewed as being sacred to Pele.

The association between hair and Pele is no mystery. During some eruptions, the wind catches molten lava as it blasts up into the air. It stretches the molten lava into individual, extremely thin threads of glass. This substance, known as "Pele's hair," often falls in abundance during eruptions. It does indeed resemble brown hair and, when seen shimmering in full sunlight on a black expanse of lava, is quite beautiful. Since Pele sent her hair to her worshippers, it only seemed fitting that they give theirs to her as offerings.

That Pele is still worshipped today as a goddess is common knowledge. Offerings of fruit, flowers, forest plants, berries, and vegetables are left to her on a daily basis at her home, Halema'uma'u. More modern offerings take the forms of bottles of gin, coins, incense, and even money. Rangers of Hawai'i's Volcanoes National Park frequently report seeing worshippers performing rites to Pele at the crater, usually at night or when others aren't about.

Pele's Loves

Pele had the normal emotional needs of any woman. Once while travelling in her spirit body, she fell in love with a young chief of Kaua'i, Lohiau. Upon returning to the island of Hawai'i, she sent her trusted sister, Hi'iaka-i-ka-poli-o-Pele, on a dangerous journey to Kaua'i to bring back her lover. Hi'iaka unfortunately fell in love with the handsome prince on her return journey, and Pele killed him twice. Each time, however, Hi'iaka restored him to life.

Another of Pele's notorious relationships was with Kamapua'ua, a famous deity who appeared in the form of a pig or a pig-man. (Kamapua'a is a *kinolau* of Lono). He enjoyed protection from the deities and widespread notoriety for his tempestuous affair with Pele.

He is said to have been born as a baby pig. In his human form, bristles could be seen down his back, betraying his pig-nature. (He sometimes wore a cape to hide the bristles.)

One day Kamapua'a appeared at the edge of Pele's home in the form of a handsome man. Pele's attendants told her of his attempts to woo her, but she would have nothing to do with him, calling him "a pig and the son of a pig."

Spurned, he taunted Pele. The two had a war of insulting words. Kamapua'a tried to approach; Pele sent her flames, tended by her volcanic brothers. Kamapua'a was nearly killed, but was saved when one of his *akua* distracted the flame-bringers (Pele's brothers) with a beautiful woman.

The fight raged on. Kamapua'a's sister brought rainstorms and fog. Hogs ran through the deluge. Pele's fires dwindled. When all but her sacred fire-sticks had been extinguished, Pele finally consented to Kamapua'a's request. They made love and her fires were restored with the fire sticks.

Pele and Kamapua'a had a child. Their relationship was both loving and violent. Eventually, Kamapua'a left her. In vain, Pele, who now loved him, tried to win him back. Though Pele has a temper, she's quite capable of giving love.

Pele Tests Her People

Pele was fond of walking as a woman among humans, and had many adventures. During one, she approached two girls in the Ka'u district of the island of Hawai'i. They were busy roasting breadfruit. Feigning hunger, she asked for food and drink. The first girl gladly gave Pele all that she desired, while the second refused, claiming that the food was dedicated to Laka.

The stingy girl's home was soon destroyed by a flood of lava, but the girl who selflessly gave of her food received a warning and was spared.

Such a sacred story, like all others, is rooted in Hawaiian culture. To refuse food to anyone, even if you were starving, was unthinkable. Just as unthinkable, however, was to visit others at meal times on a regular basis, simply to eat. Such behavior was shaming to the person's family, who might be thought of as unable to provide food.

The girl who had refused to feed Pele had not only offended the goddess, she'd broken the sacred responsibility to provide food to those

Sugar cane field, Oahu

in need. Her flimsy excuse couldn't hide her stinginess, for breadfruit isn't sacred to Laka. So she was destroyed by Pele.

Manifestations of Pele

Pele is seen today in volcanic eruptions, and sometimes in physical form. If seen dressed in white, she is warning of ill health. If in red, of impending eruptions.

Modern stories of Pele sightings continue. Perhaps the most common is a driver who stops to pick up a beautiful young woman standing by the side of the road. She gets into the car but quickly vanishes.

The Reality of Pele

Pele exists. She's a tangible, physical presence in the volcano area of the island of Hawai'i. The ground is scorched, cracked, and blackened with lava. The scent of sulfur hangs in air and irritates the throat. Steam eerily rises from the earth. During major eruptions, lava flows scorch the earth and, at the shore line, continue her ageless fight with her sister Na-maka-o-ka-ha'i as molten lava pours into the sea, causing tremendous explosions and mountains of steam.

The awesome power of Pele is a continuing source of both fear and respect for many in Hawai'i. There can be no doubt that she is, indeed, still present in the islands.

CHAPTER FIVE

Deified Ancestral Spirits

The Hawaiian concept of deity wasn't limited strictly to the *akua*. The goddesses and gods were often so awe-inspiring that their worshippers were afraid to approach them. Fortunately, a spiritual alternative existed: the *'aumakua*.

The *'aumakua* were the divine ancestors of the Hawaiian people. Each family group possessed one or many *'aumakua,* and only those directly related to a specific *'aumakua* worshipped her or him. In common with the goddesses and gods, these beings possessed great power.

The *'aumakua* are natural extensions of the strength of *ohana* (family). Families were close, even after death, and the *'aumakua* were invoked as personal deities for assistance in everyday matters.

The *'aumakua*, however, also closely watched their descendants. They favored those who were just, hard-working, and kind, warned those who were behaving badly, and punished (often by sending illness) those who broke *kapu*. These spiritual ancestors were invoked for help when one had been cursed, during sickness, or when forgiveness was desired. Different types of *'aumakua* were more helpful in assisting with specific problems.

Communication with the *'aumakua* was a part of everyday life. Though powerful and respected, these weren't the *akua;* they were

Waimea in the mist, Kaua'i

family. The *'aumakua* were invoked in prayer throughout the day, and often communicated with their descendants through dreams. *'Aumakua* could also speak directly to the family through a medium.

The *'aumakua,* in spirit form, existed in Po, a place without time or light, a "mystic sea," the underworld. When a living relative of an *'aumakua* died, his or her *'aumakua* greeted the spirit and ushered her or him into the new realm. If one wasn't greeted by one's *'aumakua,* the spirit either re-entered the body (to restore it to life), or wandered about as a ghost (see Chapter 16). One who had ignored the *'aumakua* during life might well end up as a miserable ghost *(lapu)* who wandered lonely places and ate caterpillars and spiders for food.

'Aumakua were also known to occasionally hover about the heads of their living descendants. Because of this, the head was considered to be the most sacred part of the body.

Some *'aumakua* could also be gods and goddesses. This type of *'aumakua* resulted when an *akua* and a human being mated. Children born of such unions, and their descendants, were related to the *akua* in question, and the deity was also an *'aumakua*. Ku was an *'aumakua* to some, but those not related to him recognized Ku as an god. Eventually, though, the *'aumakua* role of the major deities was largely forgotten. Additionally, some *'aumakua* became widely worshipped as deities (Pele is the best example of this). This needn't be confusing. Some divine beings were recognized as ancestors; others were not. All, however, received worship from someone.

Some families had as many as 50 or more *'aumakua,* but others apparently had none or needed more. And so rites could be performed to acquire *'aumakua*. Despite the large number of family spirits, a child was expected to memorize the names of each of her or his deified ancestors at a young age, perhaps by 7.

Kinolau

There were differences between the *akua* and *'aumakua,* and also similarities. While many images were made of deities, few were made of deified ancestral spirits. And yet both possessed *kinolau* (many bodies). Just as Pele could appear as a young woman or a flame, so too could *'aumakua* take many forms.

They could temporarily inhabit the bodies of animals, sea life, plants, and even rocks. *Kinolau* of various *'aumakua* included owls, sharks, mud hens, eels, mice, caterpillars, sea cucumbers, lizards, dogs, turtles, plovers, squid, octopi, fish, bitter gourds, sandalwood, sugar cane, bananas, coconuts, and many others.

The *'aumakua* could both help and harm. One who had a shark body could be invoked for protection at sea; an owl *'aumakua* could give protection in the forest. It was *kapu* for a family to eat or in any way interfere with any of the many bodies of their *'aumakua;* doing so would bring swift punishment. A woman who acknowledged Pele as an *'aumakua* even risked offense when walking over lava, one of Pele's bodies. The woman would ask forgiveness before stepping onto the rocks.

Shark 'Aumakua

In old Hawai'i, sharks were the ultimate symbols of strength, daring, and courage. They were feared, fierce creatures who ate humans. One famous shark was said to be thirty fathoms long, with a mouth as large as a house. Sacred stories are filled with shark wars, and many humans knew the terror of coming face to face with one of these hungry giants.

And yet, sharks could also be family members. Most (if not all) are said to have descended from one of Pele's shark brothers. (Though some state that they descended from a fierce, brave warrior who fought like a shark.) They originated in Kahiki, the Hawaiian ancestral home, and eventually came to Hawai'i. Shark *'aumakua* were recognized on all the Hawaiian islands except Kaua'i. Though usually seen in the form of sharks, they could also appear as owls, fish, lizards, or as human beings.

Shark *'aumakua* were beneficial for a people dependent upon deep-sea fishing as a source of food, and who loved to swim and surf. All of these activities held the possibility of encountering a dangerous shark. Fortunately, help was nearby: shark *'aumakua*.

These specific sharks were recognized by their markings. They enjoyed an intimate and personal relationship with their living family members, and occasionally were given offerings of pigs, chickens, and other foods. In return, the sharks guided fish into the nets, saved fishermen from drowning if their canoes capsized at sea, drove off hungry attacking sharks from swimmers, and otherwise guarded and protected their descendants.

Sometimes the shark *'aumakua* would come unbidden to lend assistance. Usually, though, the sleek-bodied ancestor would swim up at the call of an imperiled family member. Stories of shark *'aumakua* saving a drowning person by proffering a fin, allowing the worshipper to grasp it, and swimming the relative to shore are widespread. As many as 40 people are said to have been saved by one shark in a single incident.

Just as worshippers of Pele transformed their dead into spirits of Pele by throwing their bodies into the volcano, so did family members with shark *'aumakua* transform *(kaku'ai)* their dead by use of a special ritual. Offerings and prayers were made. The shark rose from the sea and opened its mouth. The deceased's family gave the shark the offerings, and finally the body, wrapped in *kapa* (bark cloth). The deceased was recognized in its new shark form by specific markings or colorings, and could be called upon in times of trouble. The new shark body of the deceased might even bear a physical resemblance to the deceased.

Not all families worshipped shark *'aumakua,* but they were quite common. Many Hawaiians never ate shark simply because to do so would be to risk eating one's ancestor. However, other families not directly related to these creatures did eat shark (though none of the varieties known for attacking human beings). They also used shark teeth to make effective weapons and shark skin for making drums.

Mo'o 'Aumakua

Another common *'aumakua* was the *mo'o. Mo'o* are lizard beings, distantly related to the innocuous gecko but of immense size. They usually lived in fishponds and were rarely seen by humans, except by family members who lit fires on altars close to the *mo'o's* home. They're described as being as much as 30 feet long and quite black in color. One of their favorite offerings is *'awa.* Lizards of all kinds were sacred to the *mo'o.* Even disturbing a lizard's nest was sufficient to ensure that the perpetrator would suffer a fall over a cliff.

Much as with sharks, families would deify their recently dead by offering them to the *mo'o.* One of the most famous of all *mo'o* worshippers and descendants was Kamehameha I, who carried out his conquest of all of Hawai'i (except for Kaua'i) in the name of his *mo'o* ancestress, Kihawahine. Kihawahine was indeed once a female chief on the island of Maui. After her death her worship also spread to Hawai'i and then to every island under Kamehameha's rule. Her image was wrapped in a yellow *kapa.*

The *mo'o* were feared by non-worshippers, as these creatures enjoyed the reputation of being fierce fighters who would stop at nothing to protect their families. Several sacred stories relate intense battles between humans and *mo'o*. Even Hi'iaka, Pele's sister, had to fight off these creatures in her quest to bring Pele's lover back from Kaua'i to her sister's spirit on Hawai'i.

Several lakes in Hawai'i are still thought to contain *mo'o*. Before safely swimming in them, the would-be bather is directed to drop a *ki* leaf or some other object in the water. The object's movement determines whether the *mo'o* is present. If so, swimming in the pool was ill-advised.

To their families, *mo'o* were loyal guardians. Fearsome, but loved.

Offending the *'Aumakua*

The *kinolau* of one's ancestors must be respected. Teasing a lizard, if done by someone related to an *'aumakua* who could take the form of a lizard, would cause the teaser to be punished by the offended *'aumakua*. Stories abound of unwise humans who offended *'aumakua*. This was why children had to learn their family's *'aumakua* and their many earthly forms early in life: to escape trouble sent by their ancestors.

The *'aumakua* were like strict but loving parents. "Remember us in prayer; leave none of us out; follow our taboos; respect our *kinolau;* take our advice" seems to have been their message. While being invoked, all of a family's *'aumakua* were individually named, the males before the females.

Today, many families still acknowledge their *'aumakua*. They may have forgotten the *akua,* but the *'aumakua* are family, and family *(ohana)* persists. This is only one step away from the Western custom of hanging pictures of long-dead ancestors on the walls, or remembering them on special events, in a form of quasi-worship. (In most Western cultures, the dead are believed to have the power to communicate with the living, particularly with relatives. This was true of old Hawai'i as well.)

The *Kupua*

When Hawaiians spoke of the "40,000 gods, the 400,000 gods, the 4,000 gods," they included in this number the *akua,* the *'aumakua,* and the *kupua.* The vast majority of these were probably the *kupua.*

Kupua were nature spirits; demi-deities or spiritual beings. Some were born of unions between humans and *akua;* others have mysterious origins. The *kupua* weren't as powerful as *akua,* nor were they related to humans as were *'aumakua.* Still, they were something more than human, and were included in all prayers, albeit in a generalized form: few were individually named.

Kupua, like *akua* and *'aumakua,* could inhabit various bodies at will: human, animal, and vegetable. They could interact with humans in these bodies.

Some *kupua* were humans who possessed great power. They were cultural heroes, and their deeds and adventures were recounted in chant and song. Even in old Hawai'i, however, many of these beings were recognized as fictional, and the accounts of their lives were entertainment. Storytelling was an art form in old Hawai'i, and specific *kupua* were often the central characters.

Many *kupua* seem to have been recognized in specific locales, and may have been unknown in others. The most famous of all *kupua* was Maui.

By their very nature, *kupua* are mysterious. Little information concerning them is available.

PART TWO

Aspects of Traditional Culture and Religion

Heiau *ruins, Big Island, Hawai'i*

CHAPTER SIX

Spiritual Power

Mana is usually defined as "spiritual power." In common with many other Hawaiian terms, this word is difficult to translate into English. *Mana* is a form of non-physical energy. This energy resides within humans, animals, plants, fish, stones, and also in certain places. It can be acquired, passed to others, taken away by the *akua*, placed into objects, and used to perform "miraculous" deeds.

All *mana* originates with the deities. They possess vast reservoirs of *mana*, far more than that which is available to mere humans. No human, while alive, has ever possessed as much *mana* as the *akua*. With this power, the gods and goddesses of Hawai'i performed both beneficial and destructive feats.

Among people, the chiefly class, as direct descendants of the deities, possessed great *mana;* so much so that it was dangerous for commoners to come into their presence. A chief who possessed remarkable leadership abilities, was physically and spiritually strong, enjoyed repeated success in battle and sport, and was quite charismatic was unusually blessed with *mana,* for it was from *mana* that these qualities were born.

The chiefs with high *mana* carefully guarded the affairs of their children. The children of chiefs married to those of other chiefs produced offspring possessed of the full *mana* of their parents. If a chief had a child with a commoner, the *mana* of this offspring would be diluted. The blood lines were therefore carefully guarded.

The chiefs weren't the only humans who possessed *mana*. Everyone (except, perhaps, the *kauwa,* or "outcasts") enjoyed the use of some *mana*.

There were two types of *mana:* that with which humans were born and that which was acquired. This first type was seen as a gift from the deities. This would be the reason for a person's extraordinary ability to do whatever she or he desired to do.

A child might have been recognized as possessing a specific type of *mana*. This child was then raised to use this *mana* in the manner dictated by the *akua:* as a carver, canoe maker, healer, farmer, sorcerer, priest, or any number of other occupations. If the child wasn't instructed in the appropriate art, the *mana* was taken back by the *akua*.

Acquired *mana* was just that—spiritual power obtained through one of several methods. Learning a craft imbued the student with *mana*. It could also be passed from one person to another.

Transferring *Mana*

Kahuna, experts in various occupations, also possessed great *mana*. This was both in-born and acquired, through intense and difficult training. Some of this *mana* was ritually passed to the *kahuna's* successor (or student) by a ritual known as *ha*. The *kahuna,* just before death, breathed into the mouth or on the top of the successor's head to pass on the *mana*. Dying people could also pass *mana* to family members.

Another form of transferring *mana* between persons was rather unusual, and we only have sacred stories to document it. This consisted of a transfer of saliva. In a story regarding Lono, who was at that time a handsome chief, a second man predicted that Lono would soon wound himself. Lono didn't believe this, but within moments he jabbed his foot with the sharp end of his digging stick. After fainting from lack of blood, Kamaka healed Lono's wound. The grateful man "begged" to become Kamaka's student. Before teaching him the power of healing herbs, Kamaka spat into Lono's mouth to lend him some of his *mana*. (For another instance of *mana* inhabiting saliva, see Chapter 17.)

Loss of *Mana*

Mana could also be lost. Misuse of skills could cause the *akua* to take back the power. This was especially true of *kahuna 'ana'ana,* the experts who killed by order of the chiefs. If these experts recklessly killed others without concern, or refused to pray to their *'ana'ana* deities, they'd soon find that their *mana* was gone.

Healing *kahuna* who ignored patients might also lose the *mana* necessary to heal. Farmers who neglected their fields could suffer *mana* loss, as could an inhumane chief. Anyone who omitted daily prayers to the *akua* and *'aumakua* also risked losing some or all of their vital spiritual power.

The *Mana* of Personal Objects

Those objects that a person used, wore, or handled during her or his lifetime were unavoidably awash with their user's personal *mana*. Even after death, some of this power ultimately remained in the hair, bones, personal possessions, and even in the deceased's name. This was one of the rationales for hiding the bones of the dead, particularly those of the chiefs, in caves.

Clothing was never shared (except by the closest relatives), because it contained the *mana* of the last person who wore it. Old clothing was usually buried or burned to prevent mixing of energies.

The *mana* that resided within personal objects was sometimes used in magic. These objects (clothing, hair, nail filings) seem to have been exclusively used for destructive magic. Personal possessions were carefully guarded to prevent the *mana* contained within them from being used to bring harm or destruction upon their owners.

Women's *Mana*

Women were considered to have vastly different *mana* than that possessed by men. This was thought to be due to menstruation. Though early (largely male and Christian) writers have stated that women in old Hawai'i were held in lower esteem due to their differing *mana,* this may not have been true. It is true that they were "forbidden" to perform many actions or to touch many objects while menstruating, but this may have been true due to the larger reserves of *mana* that were then available to them. Some contemporary writers (see Frierson, *The Burning Island: A Journey Through Myth and History in Volcano Country, Hawai'i)* speculate that men may have actually felt inadequate to women, since men couldn't give birth; nor did they experience the monthly surges of *mana* that accompanied menstruation.

These wildly powerful times may have eventually led to the many prohibitions that were placed on most women. If the women themselves couldn't control their *mana,* the men decided that they'd have to do it for them. And so women spent their menstruation each month in special one-room houses, shut off from outside contact.

Even while not menstruating, they weren't allowed within the main temples. They weren't allowed to touch the fisherman's tools and farming implements. Technically, they weren't even allowed to cook for themselves, though every woman knew how to pound *poi* and bake fish.

These prohibitions may indeed indicate that men were frightened of pre-menopausal women's greater capacity to acquire *mana* during menstruation. Lacking this ability, fearing the effects of so much uncontrolled *mana,* and feeling great envy, men may have created the special role that women held in traditional Hawaiian society.

If this theory is true, the history books of Hawai'i will have to be rewritten to show the true place of women—not as creatures despised due to their "defiling" nature, but as spiritually powerful beings who cyclically posed a threat to the male-dominated state religion and social order.

Mistaken views concerning women's role in early Hawai'i continue to be broadcast. The "expert" in traditional Hawaiian culture who informed me that women didn't pray had apparently never heard of the *hale o Papa*, the separate structure near temples in which female chiefs conducted religious services. Those people that state that women were subjugated are apparently unaware that even Kamehameha I had to enter structures occupied by one of his wives on his hands and knees, because she was of higher rank than even this great chief.

Types of *Mana* in Natural Objects

Though everyone and everything contained *mana,* Hawaiians recognized many different types of this spiritual power. Not all *mana* was identical. Indeed, in forms such as plants and fish, the precise nature of each object's *mana* widely varied. Religious and magical offerings were chosen according to their *mana,* which was often reflected in the offering's outward appearance. In medicine, those plants with *mana* that had been proven to be beneficial for specific conditions would be chosen as opposed to plants with *mana* of other kinds. Prayer was always used to enhance the effectiveness of the *mana* contained in all types of tools.

Thus, though there was only one type of power, there were in fact many types of power. Just as no two clouds are identical but share resemblances, so too was *mana* viewed in old Hawai'i. Knowing the type of *mana* contained within natural objects was of the utmost importance in all facets of life, for if objects with the incorrect *mana* were used—in any field of endeavor—the venture would not be successful.

Though probably few Hawaiians knew the *mana* of every useful plant, every food fish, every type of stone, and all other natural objects, experts *(kahuna)* certainly knew the tools of their profession.

Na Pali coast, Kaua'i

Part of the training of all experts was memorization of the specific influences that could be expected through the use of specific objects.

In the past, a man about to make a canoe would select a tree with suitable *mana:* it would be straight, tall, resistant to cracking, strong enough to maintain its shape, and not so heavy that it would sink when placed on the water. These were outward manifestations of the *mana* contained within the tree.

When a new house was to be built, fish of the *'aholehole* type were placed beneath each post to protect the home (Titcomb, p. 60). Another type of fish wouldn't have been as effective, for only the *'aholehole* possessed the correct type of *mana* (in this case, the ability to "strip away" evil influences).

Today, a highly skilled auto mechanic would be admired for his ability to choose the tools with the correct *mana* to repair a car. A doctor who prescribed effective medicines would similarly be praised for her or his knowledge of *mana*. Though Hawaiians had different tools and had a different understanding of their natures, they were just as proficient with them, in large part because of their training.

The specific type of *mana* contained within natural objects was of great importance in everyday life, in religion, and in magic.

Moving *Mana*

Mana was moved into objects. This was sometimes performed by the *akua*, who then gave the magically empowered object to a person to assist her or him with problems. Some *kahuna* could also imbue an object with *mana*. This was done through a process that we know as magic. The *kahuna aloha* (expert in love magic) would empower a piece of sugar cane with loving *mana;* the *kahuna la'au lapa'au* increased the *mana* of healing plants, which were then given to the patient; the *kahuna 'ana'ana* sent destructive *mana* into a piece of wood, which then killed. The movement of *mana* was magic (See Chapter 17).

Mana is, by its very nature, a mysterious force. To the Hawaiians, it was a gift from the *akua* and *'aumakua*, who lent it to all persons and things.

Magic was a use of *mana*. So too was sailing great distances, jumping off high cliffs, predicting the weather, praying to the deities, making bark cloth, planting sweet potatoes, surfing twenty-foot waves, diagnosing and treating illnesses with herbs and massage, fishing, carving images of the *akua*, running, conceiving a child, giving birth, fighting in battle, catching birds, wrestling, making fish hooks, designing temples, flying kites in fighting contests, sledding down hills, and teaching and learning new skills. No part of life in old Hawai'i was divorced from *mana*.

If, today, we view *mana* simply as talent, initiative, determination, and application of skills, we have far less than a true picture of spiritual power. Behind and beyond these outward manifestations lies that which allows them to occur—spiritual power, a gift from the deities.

CHAPTER SEVEN

Taboos

Kapu. The word is still heard in Hawai'i today almost two centuries after it was officially abandoned by King Liholiho in 1819.

Kapu (taboos) were religious and civil prohibitions and privileges. Some were universally applicable; others pertained only to members of specific families and professions. Additionally, actions that were at some times *kapu* were free of taboo at others. Many applied only to women.

Kapu was a vital part of traditional Hawaiian religion, for most of these restrictions were linked with the deities. Even those forms of *kapu* that don't seem to be connected with spirituality are often in some way connected either with the deities or with *mana*.

Types of *Kapu*

Ali'i Kapu

The chiefly class, as possessors of great *mana,* were subject to many *kapu,* most of which dictated their actions as well as the actions of the few commoners with whom they came into contact.

Virtually everything belonging to chiefs was *kapu* to the commoners. Wearing a chief's loincloth was punishable by death, as was handling anything belonging to the chiefs (such as mats, *kapa,* and pillows), or entering *ali'i* territory.

Another unique *kapu* concerned a chief's shadow. Because a person's shadow contained some of his or her *mana,* it was forbidden for any commoner to cross the shadow of an *ali'i.* Similarly, if a commoner's shadow fell on a chief's house, he or she had also broken *kapu.*

The highest-born of the *ali'i* enjoyed what was known as the prostrating *kapu.* When a person of this status approached, the people knelt, sat, or threw themselves on the ground, according to the severity of the *kapu* (which was determined by the chief's rank). Such *kapu* were often of as great a burden to the chiefs as they were to the common people.

Women's Kapu

Many *kapu* pertained exclusively to women. The *kapu* of the *akua* decreed that women weren't permitted to eat with men, cook their own food, touch fishing equipment, or enter the temples.

Women's food *kapu (ʻai kapu)* are among the most famous. Forbidden to them were the coconut (a form of Ku, and never extremely abundant), all varieties of bananas save for two types (the banana is a form of Kanaloa and wasn't particularly relished as food), several types of fish used in rituals (such as the *ulua* and *kumu*), and the manta ray, sea turtle, and whale (all forms of Kanaloa).

Pork was forbidden to women, as it was used in sacrifices to the deities. Other foods, such as shark, were reserved for the *ali'i* (only those that didn't have a shark *'aumakua*). Only women of the highest rank could ever eat such foods, and then only in extraordinary situations.

Some say that these food prohibitions were instituted in the past when the birth rate was growing to such an alarming extent that overpopulation threatened continued human existence on these small islands. Women were forced to observe a less nourishing diet to slow the birth rate. Others say that these food *kapu* were designed to have the opposite effect: to increase the birth rate by strengthening women's reproductive abilities.

Ecological Kapu

Fish provided a major source of protein for Hawaiians. Two fish in particular, the *'opelu* and the *aku*, were of such importance that they were cyclically protected. A *kapu* was placed upon catching these fish while they were spawning, to ensure their continuing supply in the future.

Particularly rich fishing grounds were similarly protected with year-round *kapu* to prevent overfishing. One place would be *kapu* for a month, then the *kapu* was lifted and another place would be taboo. Seaweed (seen as fish food) was similarly protected. Specific types of fish were also *kapu* to catch or to eat during certain months of the year.

Such far-sighted ecological measures were common in old Hawai'i. Groves of trees were placed under *kapu* when needed. Off-limits areas were often marked by two crossed sticks, the tops of which were wrapped with *kapa* (bark cloth). These were known as *bulo'ulo'u*. Such *kapu* were temporary and all understood the importance of these prohibitions.

Perhaps one of the most sensible of all the taboos was the prohibition against bathing or washing in any stream except at its mouth. This preserved the cleanliness of the Hawaiians' major sources of drinking water.

Wailua Falls, Kaua'i

Sound Kapu

During certain ceremonies, particularly the dedication of war temples, sound of any kind was *kapu*. Dogs and chickens were covered with gourds to silence them and children were trained to keep quiet. Words and all sounds were conduits of power; therefore, they had to be carefully controlled during solemn rituals.

Occupational Kapu

While learning or practicing a craft or special skill, its practitioners were often forbidden to eat certain foods or behave in certain ways. Most occupations (farming, dance, carving, magic, healing) were learned and practiced under *kapu*.

Fishing had its unique share of *kapu*. Women were forbidden to touch fishing hooks, fishing lines, nets, octopus lures, or any other equipment of the fisherman. The fisherman's mate couldn't have sex while he was out fishing, nor could his family fight or the fisherman's bait be eaten. Some fishermen never wore red, the color of Ku'ula (the fishing deity), and forbade the presence of bananas on board their outrigger canoes. Some of these *kapu* were religious, others were personal. The legion of prohibitions associated with fishing illuminates the importance of fish in the diet of the early Hawaiians.

Clothing Kapu

It was *kapu* to wear the clothing of any other than the closest family members. Once clothing had been worn, it was buried or burned so that no one else could wear it. This also safeguarded it from being used in negative magical operations against its original wearer.

Household Kapu

Sleeping mats were used only for sleeping. Pillows (made of woven *lauhala*) weren't footstools; only one's head ever reclined on them.

Cyclical Kapu

The Hawaiian calendar was based on the lunar month. Each day was auspicious for certain activities, or inauspicious for others. Many were *kapu* to certain deities, and on these days specific actions were forbidden. (See the Appendix.) These *kapu*, created during the time of the primordial god Wakea, are among the oldest.

'Aumakua Kapu

Families related to sharks, turtles, coconut, breadfruit, sweet potatoes, and other creatures and plants used as food were forbidden to eat them, for to do so would be to risk consuming an ancestor. Similarly, unduly disturbing or harming one's 'aumakua was prohibited. Such kapu were unquestioned.

Kapu Originally not so Severe

The kapu that was in force in old Hawai'i seems to have undergone major changes with the arrival of the Tahitian priest Pa'ao in the 1200s. Originally, kapu were far less severe and complex and, thus, were easier to follow. Most related solely to the deities. Commoners and chiefs freely mingled, and the temples were open to both men and women.

This changed. Gone were the days of easy living; kapu multiplied and increased to the extent that life became perilous, for it was difficult for word of each of these new kapu to reach all persons. Many fled to the pu'uhonua (place of refuge; see Chapter 9) after discovering that they'd unwittingly broken a kapu.

Cruel chiefs ordered cruel or meaningless kapu, such as the one that required all canoes to lower their sails while travelling near a specific shore of an island. Fortunately such chiefs were few, and Hawaiian history recounts tales of unjust chiefs being put to death by outraged people.

Punishment

Punishment for breaking kapu was usually death. However, a chief could pronounce a kanawai, an edict that spared the life of the transgressor. The ali'i were forced by circumstances to lead rather solitary lives; the chiefs could rarely leave their sacred compounds and mingle with the common people, save in disguise. Punishment for such infractions seems to have been rare or nonexistent.

Because so many of the kapu were created by the deities, divine retribution often followed if one was deliberately broken. Even if no human eyes saw the transgressor's misdeed, the deity would usually swiftly sent death.

Kapu, then, was a rigid collection of behavioral rules handed down from both the *akua* and the *ali'i.* Many of them, such as regulating the taking of coconuts from a grove threatened by over-harvesting, are quite sensible to our ecologically-aware minds. Others may seem meaningless, but Hawaiians had good reasons for everything that they did. Their world view is simply too different for us to understand.

The End of the *Kapu*

By 1819, the Hawaiians had become well acquainted with the manners of Western civilization. The whaling, exploring, and trading ships that frequently anchored in the islands' bays were filled with people who broke every *kapu* without suffering any consequences.

Observation of this fact, misty news of these strangers' "new" religion, and Kamehameha I's widow (and favorite wife) Ka'ahumanu, who was tiring of the *kapu,* led to the overthrow of the system on October 4, 1819, when a much-goaded King Liholiho (Kamehameha II) publicly sat and ate with women—breaking one of the oldest and most fundamental of all *kapu.*

Runners spread the word throughout the islands: the *kapu* system had been abolished and, with it, the old religion. Temples were ordered destroyed. Images of the deities were burned. State religious rituals ended.

But this didn't mean the end of traditional religion in Hawai'i. *Kahuna pule* (prayer priests) continued to practice their rites. Persons still privately prayed to their *'aumakua.* Workers in most professions honored the *akua* connected with their crafts.

With the arrival of the first missionaries in 1820, the old religion had waned in popularity, and only in secret could the rites continue to be performed under the far-reaching (and culturally devastating) influence of the Christians who had come to "assist" the "savages."

CHAPTER EIGHT

Experts: The Kahuna

Many of those who have heard of *kahuna* think of them only as evil magicians who prayed others to death. Actually, the above statement is true of only a tiny fraction of *kahuna*. *Kahuna* were experts of all kinds trained and fully prepared to carry out the duties of their offices. They were the keepers of all knowledge in old Hawai'i.

There were *kahuna* dedicated to specific deities—of crafts, healing, architecture, navigation, canoe building, omen reading, sports—the list includes all areas of life in ancient Hawai'i. To a certain extent, all were priests as well, for religion infused every aspect of life.

These men—and some women—were often singled out at birth or in infancy, and raised to fulfill their promise. Though usually of the *ali'i* (chiefly class), some commoners found to possess exceptional *mana* could also become *kahuna*.

Types of *Kahuna*

The most difficult type of *kahuna* to become was the *kahuna nui*. Such persons were expert in all things: they could heal and (if necessary) pray a person to death, could carve a canoe and navigate it across the ocean, recite extremely long genealogical chants from memory, design a temple, fish, and grow crops. They also counselled the chiefs, and had to be *ali'i* themselves. Such *kahuna* were rare and were usually of advanced age, for training in so many professions was the work of a lifetime.

The *kahuna pule* (literally, "prayer experts") were the priests who attended to religious duties. They, too, were of the *ali'i*. Sometimes they were attached to a specific temple at which they led a variety of rituals, depending on the type of temple (see Chapter 9). They had many other duties in service to the people, including blessing a newly constructed house and cleansing those who had been defiled by contact with corpses. Many *kahuna pule* were devoted to a specific goddess or god. Ku, Kane, and Lono had orders of priests, as probably did many other deities.

Healing was an important part of early life, and there were many types of *kahuna* healers, just as there are a myriad of branches of the healing profession today. These experts included *kahuna la'au lapa'au* (medicinal herbal healer), *kahuna ha'iha'i iwi* (bone-setting expert), *kahuna haha* (diagnostician), *kahuna ho'ohanau* (midwife), and, among many others, the *kahuna lomilomi*, who used powerful massage and steam baths as curative agents.

Carvers of the sacred images of the deities were known as *kahuna kalai*, while those who were expert canoe carvers were *kahuna kalai wa'a*. The navigators who guided the canoes were known as *kahuna ho'okelewa'a*. Agricultural experts, who were proficient in every aspect of planting, were *kahuna ho'oulu 'ai*. Sites for new temples, fishponds, and houses, as well as the designs for them, were selected by the *kahuna kuhikuhipu'uone*.

The lovesick could visit the *kahuna aloha* for magical rites to draw their beloved and the *kahuna ho'ohapai keiki* for ritual assistance in becoming pregnant. The *kahuna pale keiki* determined the sex of the child and the day of birth, and was also an expert in childbirth. If necessary or desired, a *kahuna* could also be consulted for medical abortive procedures.

The *kahuna kilo* observed the skies for omens of the future; the *kahuna kilo hoku,* the stars; the *kahuna kilo honua* watched the earth for signs; the *kahuna nana uli* predicted the weather. Additionally, some general prophets were known as *kahuna kaula* (though other prophets weren't *kahuna;* see Chapter 18).

The most famous *kahuna* were the sorcerer experts: the *kahuna 'ana'ana* prayed others to death on orders of the ruling chief, the *kahuna ho'opi'opi'o* caused distress or sickness by concentration and gesture, and the *kahuna ho'ounauna* sent spirits flying on destructive missions.

This brief look at just a few of the types of *kahuna* should serve to demonstrate that they weren't simply a class of sorcerous magicians. *Kahuna* were respected persons who had been trained to be adept in specific professions. Today, doctors, surgeons, architects, teachers, engineers, priests and priestesses, psychiatrists, computer programmers, sculptors, midwives, electricians—all would be considered to be *kahuna* (experts).

Women as *Kahuna*

Information concerning female *kahuna* is difficult to obtain. There certainly were some female *kahuna* (known as *kahuna wahine)* who were experts in various professions, but whether this was standard practice at all times and in all districts of each island is impossible to determine.

Kahuna pule wahine (female prayer experts) were recognized, and these women sometimes prayed in the temple (usually the domain of male *kahuna*). These women were always of the chiefly class. When they entered the temple they wore a *malo kea* (white loincloth), an article of clothing usually reserved for men. (White was also a color often worn by *kahuna pule.)* While menstruating, however, even women *kahuna* were forbidden to enter the *heiau.*

Some women also became famous as *kaula* (prophets) and were known as *kaula wahine.* Whether some were recognized as *kahuna* or not is difficult to determine.

What seems most likely is that many women were, indeed, experts in their fields, even if they didn't receive the honor of being named *kahuna.* Chiefesses as well as chiefs loved to surf, dance, sled down hills on thin wooden sleds, and perform many other sports. Hawaiian sacred stories are filled with women competing against men in these activities. Since there were male *kahuna* who were experts in such sports as spear throwing (a pastime commonly played to ensure accuracy during battle), wrestling, and probably in all other sports, it seems possible that some women were recognized as *kahuna* of certain sports. This remains, however, speculation.

Training of the *Kahuna*

A child who was recognized as possessing a natural talent for a specific craft or profession was raised to it and most became *kahuna.* This was a recognition of the child's specific *mana.* No one could be born a *kahuna;* this title was achieved solely through training and application of studies. Some sources state that *kahuna* were trained for 20 years before "graduating," but the length of time required was probably determined by the type of profession. At times older persons also approached *kahuna* for teaching.

Before training could begin, the candidate or his family made gifts to the *kahuna* teacher. These included pigs, fine sleeping mats, and other valuables. Such gifts were necessary and can be viewed as a form of tuition.

Some training was undertaken in special schools, such as the healing school believed to have once been situated near Keaiwa *heiau* in Aiea near Honolulu. Other times a promising child would be guided by a single *kahuna* who would welcome the apprentice as a houseguest during training.

The first lessons were the prayers. These were the foundation of all work in all professions, and had to be perfectly memorized. True faith in and certain knowledge of the powers and existence of the *akua* was necessary; those trainees who were observed to lack religious conviction were denied further training.

Prayer was so important because it was through prayer (and other actions, but specifically prayer) that the *kahuna* sent *mana*. Prayer enhanced the effectiveness of all types of work precisely because it moved *mana*. Traditional prayers therefore had to be perfectly memorized, and not one word could be changed while they were being said.

After the prayers the *kapu* (taboos) of the attendant deity were learned. These were of tremendous importance, for breaking the profession's titular deity's *kapu* would render all workings ineffective and would bring the wrath of the deity upon the student.

Finally, basic instruction began. Training methods could be difficult. They were often under *kapu* which forbade the students any outside activities not related to their lessons.

Questions were usually not encouraged; everything that was needed to be learned would be demonstrated by the *kahuna,* in sometimes oblique ways. The student was expected to listen to the words of the teacher, observe everything, and constantly learn. Since there were no books in old Hawai'i, observation was the most efficient method of learning.

Stories are still whispered about some of the harsh teaching methods. Great physical, emotional, and mental demands might be placed upon the student, who was expected to face anything with power *(mana)*, patience, and complete faith in the tutelary deity governing the profession being studied. Some other lessons weren't dangerous but simply difficult to master. The *kahuna haha*-in-training, who diagnosed by feeling the body of the patient, was taught to recognize hundreds of diseases by touch alone.

After the successful completion of studies, the students graduated and were considered to be *kahuna*. Graduation from a specific training program was often but the first phase of studies. A new course of lessons might follow in a related or unrelated profession. A *kahuna kilo* might learn next of the signs from the stars, the earth, and the weather, thus becoming proficient in four aspects of divination, his chosen profession.

A *kahuna la'au lapa'au* (herbal healer) might learn the art of diagnosing disease by touch or sight, so that he or she could both determine the problem and correct it with herbal remedies. This could be followed up with study in *lomilomi* (massage).

One rule governed the *kahuna:* never do anything for which you weren't trained. Thus, many *kahuna* widened their knowledge so that they didn't break this rule.

As we've seen, *kahuna* were experts in many fields. They were the keepers of knowledge—the advisors and counselors and craftspersons and priests. Though much of their wisdom has been lost, sparks of it still exist within those who are reviving the ancient arts and crafts of Hawai'i, and people calling themselves *kahuna* can still be found today.

CHAPTER NINE

Temples and Shrines

Jumbled piles of lava stones. Rocky platforms gleaming blackly in the sun. Fitted stone walls and graceful terraces. Massive constructions built by human hands with countless thousands of stones that may have been transported for many miles. Perched on cliffs facing the sea ... hidden in valleys ... standing beside fields.

The *heiau* (temples or sacred places) of old Hawai'i were once quite numerous. Each district of each island had many: *heiau* for healing, for war, for rain, for agriculture. There were weather *heiau;* those that served as schools; *heiau* built for peace. Additionally, small shrines also peppered the islands. During the first three decades of this century, more than 800 *heiau* and shrines were discovered and catalogued by researchers.

Many of these have since been destroyed, victims of the development of the Hawaiian islands. Some lie hidden in dense brush; many survive only in ruins. A few have been carefully restored. Some of them today once again hear ancient chants and feel the tread of feet on their sacred stones during secret nighttime rituals. Virtually all known remaining temples still receive offerings. A look at these dramatic monuments of ancient Hawaiian spirituality gives us an insight into the nature of the old ways.

Shrines

Shrines were by far the most common places of worship. They were usually quite compact; their construction required no priests or architects, and massive human power was unnecessary to build them. Anyone could create a shrine and worship the deity for whom it was built. A shrine differed from a *heiau* only in its size and purpose.

Family Shrines

The simplest form of *heiau* was the *Pohaku o Kane:* "Stone of Kane." As its name suggests, this stone was dedicated to Kane. It was an elongated stone from one to six feet in length, usually waterworn, that was set upright within the family's household complex and served as the family shrine. Many families had a *Pohaku o Kane,* which was often planted around with *ki* (see Chapter 13).

This was where male family members would go to pray to their *'aumakua* for health, forgiveness for broken *kapu,* for good crops, and unending food supplies. Women and girls apparently didn't pray at the *Pohaku o Kane.* Offerings of food and *'awa* were made by the family to Kane at this stone. Archaeologists investigating ancient living sites have found *Pohaku o Kane* surrounded by coral; perhaps coral was also offered there.

Not just any stone could be used as the *Pohaku o Kane.* Such a stone was pointed out by Kane during a dream or a vision. The family itself set up the stone and performed simple rituals to create the *Pohaku o Kane.* No *kahuna* was called for assistance.

Some say that the Stone of Kane was placed within the *hale mua* (men's eating house), and served as the altar. Others say that it was on the grounds of the household but not within any structure. Most agree, however, that the *Pohaku o Kane* was where the men and boys worshipped on a daily basis.

Other family shrines might have been made. These usually consisted of a small thatched structure surrounded by either a low stone wall or a wooden fence. In this house was a small altar made of wood and greenery, and it was here that the family kept their *'aumakua* images and the *ipu-o-Lono* (see Chapter 3). However, this structure might have been the men's eating house *(mua);* much is unclear.

Fishing Shrines

Fishing shrines *(ko'a)* were extremely common in coastal areas and riverbanks near rich fishing areas. They could consist of anything from a simple flat rock upon which offerings were placed to small stone platforms in rectangular or circular form. These were made to ensure bountiful catches of fish and other sea creatures.

The *ko'a ku'ula ho'oulu i'a* (usually shortened to *ko'a*) was the site of offerings to Ku'ula, a fishing god. He was often represented by a stone that, through natural erosion and shaping by the ocean, resembled a fish (See Chapter 11). Offerings were made before setting out to fish, and the first catch of the day was often laid on a flat stone at the shrine. Other offerings made at *ko'a* included coral, crabs, sea urchins, and mollusks. Not surprisingly, fishhooks have also been found on these shrines.

Though each *ko'a* was dedicated to one deity alone, usually Ku'ula, two fishing shrines were often built side by side. The second *ko'a* was often dedicated to Hinahele, a fishing goddess who was worshipped by both women and fishermen, and to whom *'ohua* (fish spawn) were sacred.

Another type of fishing shrine, *ko'a ho'oulu 'o'opu,* was erected near fresh water streams, lakes, and fishponds to increase the abundance of the *'o'opu* fish, a prized food. Rituals there were performed to Holu, a god of this fish, or to Kaneko'a, a form of Kane. *Ko'a* dedicated to the increase of other types of fish were also created.

Ko'a throughout the islands still bear offerings of fish. I've seen fresh fish and the bones of earlier offerings on *ko'a* on the Island of Hawai'i. Even today, such offerings apparently increase in number during periods of unfruitful fishing.

Path Shrines

Path shrines were found in many places, particularly in hills. They usually consisted of simple upright stones or a small stone platform. Since each district was governed by different deities and spirits, it was deemed appropriate by those travelling from one district to another to leave an offering at the shrine. Leaves, stones, or other objects would be laid on the shrine to placate the spirits. This was quite important while travelling in dangerous areas; failure to leave an offering could result in becoming lost, injured, or killed by the offended spirits.

Occupational Shrines

Because each occupation was presided over by one or more attendant deities, small shrines existed for each profession. Bird catchers (who gathered feathers), farmers, woodcutters, and men and women of every occupation gave sacrifice at their appropriate shrines. Offerings and prayers designed to ensure success were made before work began each day.

Fertility Shrines

At one time every island had a fertility shrine, which usually consisted of a single upright stone that resembled the male genitalia. Infertile women, wishing to conceive, would bring offerings to these places and spend the night at the base of the stone. They were usually pregnant by the next morning. Other female stones were often nearby (See Chapter 11).

Precisely which *akua* were worshipped there and at other stones of this nature is unclear. It may have been Ku.

Heiau

Heiau are large temple complexes. They were built at the orders of the ruling chief, and their construction was a district-wide occupation; the workers of an entire island never came together to create one of these temples. Thousands of workers carried and placed stones according to the design created by the *kahuna kuhikuhi pu'uone* (architect). The last *heiau* built, Pu'ukohola on the Island of Hawai'i, stretches on a hill above the sea for an incredible length and rises to an impressive height.

What could such a temple have in common with a pile of stones used by fishermen to increase their catches and to thank their deities? *Heiau* are elaborate versions of the simple shrines, suitable for more complex rituals. As places of sacrifice and offering, both shrines and *heiau* were crucially important to traditional Hawaiian religion.

The first *heiau* built in Hawai'i probably resembled the temples of Tahiti (known there as *marae*). These were simple stone-paved courtyards or plazas, often surrounded by a low wall. The altar was usually a raised platform (also of stone) surrounded by a semi-circle of images of the deities. According to tradition, no human sacrifices were made within these earliest *heiau*.

As Hawaiian civilization progressed, however, *heiau* grew more complex. New designs and styles were created that were far more complex than those made in Tahiti. Then, in the twelfth century, a powerful priest named Pa'ao arrived in Hawai'i from Tahiti and directed that huge *luakini* (human sacrifice) temples be built to honor the god that he had brought. The *heiau* was on its way to becoming one of the most awe-inspiring structures in the entire Pacific region.

Basic Plan of Heiau

Incredible variation existed in *heiau*; in fact, no two were alike. So many were built that their architecture became a profession. Temple architects *(kahuna kuhikuhi nu'uone)* knew every *heiau* on the island and would create variations on the designs of older temples. Architects made models of proposed temples by molding them from wet sand. These models of the *heiau's* finished design were then shown to the chief who had ordered the temple's construction.

Most *heiau* weren't permanently tended. After they'd been constructed, the proper rituals had been performed, and the blessings had been received, the temple might be abandoned until it was again needed, at which time it was refitted and repaired. Alternately, a new *heiau* could be built on the site of an older temple; indeed, this was the only suitable spot for erecting some types of *heiau*.

Though variations occur, some generalities can be made here about the basic plan of *heiau*. They were constructed of the strongest available material: lava rock. The rocks were chosen for their specific *mana,* which was determined in part by their size, shape, and place of origin. Rocks were often moved many miles to be used in the construction of a *heiau*.

More information regarding *luakini* (human sacrifice) temples is available than that of other types of *heiau,* and the following information describes this form of temple.

Heiau usually consisted of a square or rectangular area enclosed by a low rock wall. A raised platform was usual at one end of this courtyard. The floor of the enclosure was covered with smooth stones for ease of walking within its precincts. If the temple was built on a hillside, the stones were piled up until they created a flat surface. On it were several buildings, depending on the type of *heiau*.

In a typical *heiau,* such buildings consisted of an *anu'u* tower, a tall structure (perhaps 24 feet high) made of strong timber and covered with *kapa*. This three-story structure served several purposes. Offerings were made on the first story. The second saw rituals performed by the *kahuna pule* or *kahuna nui* and his assistants. The third story was sacrosanct; only the ruling chief and *kahuna* could tread there. Here the *akua* took possession of the chief or *kahuna* and, through him, revealed the future. It was this last usage that caused the *anu'u* to be termed an "oracle tower."

A *lele* (offering stand) was also present in all *heiau*. This was a simple upright stand created of one, two, or four legs that supported a platform on which offerings of fruit, *lei,* vegetables, and pigs were laid.

Other structures found in *heiau* included a *hale pahu* (drum house), *hale imu* (oven house, in which fires were started and food cooked for offerings), and the *hale mana (mana* house). The *luakini heiau* had a special feature: the *luakini* ("pit of 40,000," referring to the

Heiau, *Big Island, Hawai'i*

sacrifices placed there). The woods used to create these buildings were also dependent on the temple's type.

Semi-circular arrangements of large *ki'i* (wooden images of the *akua*) were also present in most *luakini heiau*. At times, these partially surrounded the *lele*.

Outside, but near the entrance to the *heiau,* were the female *akua* (goddess) images and an additional *lele* stand. Perhaps these were used by women, who were forbidden to enter the *heiau*. (See also *Hale o Papa* below.)

Types of Heiau

Among the types of *heiau* were the *mapele heiau*, those dedicated to Lono. They were benign temples where only offerings of food and pigs were made; human sacrifice never occurred within their walls. Presided over by the priests of Lono, rites within the *mapele* were concerned with blessing the crops, giving thanks for bountiful harvests, and other peaceful purposes (Malo p. 9). Those built for agricultural purposes

were collectively known as *heiau unuunu ho'ouluai*. Similar temples
were used in the worship of Kane.

For people who travelled far on the open sea to other islands or
to distant fishing places, safety while sailing was a primary concern.
Before leaving on a long voyage, a *na ko'a heiau holomoana* was built
to ensure the deities would be of assistance during their dangerous
voyages.

During times of drought and famine, rain temples were erected.
Such temples were hastily built and then dismantled. They had a single function: to plead with the *akua* to bring rain. One famous rain
temple was in Nu'uanu Valley, O'ahu. Since rain is necessary for agricultural abundance, these *heiau* were of the class known as *heiau ho'o
uluulu 'ai*. Another type of *heiau (kalua ua)* was built to halt torrential
rains, which could be as destructive to the food supply as was drought.
Within such temples, rainwater was wrapped in *ki* leaves and baked in
underground ovens to stop the rain.

Medical *kahuna* often worked in a *heiau ho'ola* (healing temple).
Here they worshipped their deities, treated patients, taught the healing
arts, and grew medicinal plants. There was once one healing temple in
each district on every island; today, Keaiwa in the Aiea area of O'ahu
is the best known example. (See the end of this chapter.)

The *heiau loulu* was a temporary structure created from a wooden
framework thatched with the large leaves of the *loulu* palm. It was built
to promote an abundance of fish.

Hale o Papa

Since women (even chiefesses) weren't normally permitted to enter the
sacred precincts of the *heiau*, they worshipped outside the walled temple on land that was still considered to be sacred.

Early historians failed to record much information regarding the
Hale o Papa ("House of the Goddess Papa") since they were fascinated
by the male-dominated rites of the *luakini heiau*. Still, we have a few
clues about these goddess temples.

The House of Papa was apparently a small house-like structure set on a rock flooring and surrounded with rock walls. The *Hale o Papa* at Waha'ula *heiau* on the Island of Hawai'i was measured as 23 by 33 feet with stone walls.

According to Kamakau, high ranking chiefesses worshipped within the House of Papa. Papa may have been among those goddesses who received offerings in the *Hale o Papa*. It has been stated by an early writer that this was a "comfortable" *heiau:* they were less stringent than those of the *luakini heiau*.

The nature of the worship that occurred within the *Hale o Papa* is little known. Offerings of pigs and *kapa* (bark cloth) were made at regular intervals. Upon occasion, the district's ruling chief visited to participate in ceremonies, and there are mentions of priests of Pele entering the house as well. Usually, however, it seems to have been reserved for worship by women.

Pu'uhonua

Pu'uhonua were literally places of refuge. These were areas of peace, safety, and life. It was to these sanctuaries that the *kapu* breaker, the defeated soldier, and all those in spiritual crisis would run in times of need. The grounds of such *heiau* were so sacred that even those about to be put to death for their crimes, or soldiers from defeated armies, were spared if they could reach a *pu'uhonua* before being captured.

The priests who attended the *pu'uhonua* performed elaborate purification rituals on those that came to them. Once cleansed, such people could safely return to normal life, and no reparation could be made against them, even by the highest chief. Their past crimes were forgotten.

Defeated soldiers, the elderly, maimed and crippled people, and children were sheltered within the *pu'uhonua* during times of battle. Enemy soldiers respected this tradition and never trespassed onto the sacred ground, nor attacked these places of refuge.

Part of the power of these *pu'uhonua* came from the bones of deceased chiefs that were kept in the *heiau* that formed part of every *pu'uhonua.* Such bones continued to emit *mana* and, since chiefs enjoyed great amounts of *mana* during life, they blessed the area with great spiritual power.

In the past, *pu'uhonua* were common; at least one existed within each island district. Actually entering such sanctuaries was sometimes difficult, for they might be surrounded by homes of the *ali'i* (near which commoners could not tread), high stone walls, *heiau* (*kapu* to commoners), and the ocean. Others were quite open, not surrounded by walls and easily reached—if the transgressors could race to them in time.

The most famous of these places of refuge, Pu'uhonua O Honaunau in the South Kona district of Hawai'i, has been restored and is a National Historic Park. Even today it's a place of peace and serenity, with the blue Pacific lapping a small coral sand beach and coconut trees shading the visitor from the burning Kona sun.

The tradition of the *pu'uhonua* was of ancient origin and is another example of the largely humane nature of early Hawaiians.

Heiau Today

Many *heiau* have been lost, but some can still be visited today. Some are on private land, others on public land, and still others have been transformed into parks. Just a few of the famous *heiau* on each the major islands are listed below.

Kaua'i

The area just above Ke'e beach, at the end of the road, is rich in archaeological sites. Ka-ulu-o-Laka *heiau* was a temple for *hula* dancers (*'olapa*). Nearby is the Ka-ulu-Paoa, commemorating the place where Lohi'au (a young chief whom Pele loved) trained in *hula* with his friend Paoa. It is the former of these that *hula* students try to visit at least once during their lives. They leave offerings to Laka, goddess of the *hula,* at this place. (At this site, Pele, in her spirit body, fell in love with the handsome chief Lohi'au.)

Maui

Pihana Kalani *heiau* is a *luakini heiau* in Wailuku. Traditionally, it was built by a group *of menehune* (see Chapter 15) during a single night. Others say that it was erected by Chief Kahekili. (This *heiau* is also known as Haleki'i, or image house.) Little is known about it and it's in disrepair.

O'ahu

Keaiwa *heiau*, near Aiea, is an old healing *heiau*. It is now a state park, and it is still a peaceful and healing place far above the bustle of Honolulu. A cool breeze blows there and many still visit to ask for healings.

Ulu Po *heiau* near Kailua is one of many temples said to have been built by *menehune* during a single night. This large, open platform, situated on a hillside, is still an impressive structure.

Above Waimea Bay is Pu'u o Mahuka *heiau,* the largest in existence on O'ahu. This was a *luakini* (human sacrifice) *heiau* and many today refuse to visit it because of its disturbing *mana.* Its extreme age has again been responsible for crediting the *menehune* as its builders.

Hawai'i

Ahu'ena *heiau* (on the grounds of the King Kamehameha Hotel in Kona) is a ¾-sized reconstruction of the original temple that stood there. Kamehameha I restored it and used it for worship.

Mo'okini *heiau,* situated on the northern tip of the island in Kohala, is a famous *luakini* temple dedicated to Ku. Said to have been first constructed in 500 CE and later reconstructed by Pa'ao in about 1200 CE, it's said to be still cared for by the same family whose ancestors ordered it built.

Pu'uhonua O Honaunau, located in the South Kona district, is an ancient place of refuge. A trip through the grounds (the area is now a National Historic Park) is quite informative. Features include three *heiau,* massive stone walls, fish ponds, and wondrous modern recreations of *akua ki'i* (god images). The beach laps near the Hale o Keawe, the best reconstructed temple site in Hawai'i.

Pu'ukohola, located about an hour's drive north of Kailua-Kona, is a massive, elongated temple built in the late 1700s by Kamehameha I on advice from a prophet, who predicted that building the temple would ensure Kamehameha's desire to bring all of the Hawaiian islands under his control. Built on the site of an earlier *heiau,* another, older temple is situated just below Pu'ukohola.

Wahaula Heiau, in the Puna district, is traditionally the first temple built on orders of the Tahitian priest Pa'ao, and the first that required human sacrifice. Unfortunately, recent flows from the East Rift vents of Kilauea have destroyed the visitor's center built here, and, by the time you read this, may have completely covered over Wahaula *heiau,* as the flows have destroyed a nearby popular swimming spot (the Queen's Bath), numerous homes, black sand beaches, miles of forest, and parts of the Chain of Craters road.

Pu'ukohola Heiau

CHAPTER TEN

Water

To the Hawaiians, water was a gift from the *akua;* the unending source of *ola* (life). It fell from the sky, bubbled mysteriously up from the earth, ran in silvery-white rivulets down the sides of steep cliffs, and languorously made its way to the ocean in the many streams that grace the islands.

Reliable sources of fresh water are necessary for human life. Had the major Hawaiian islands been bereft of such sources, they never would have been populated. The great importance given to water in Hawai'i can be easily demonstrated: the Hawaiian word for wealth, abundance, and prosperity, *waiwai,* is simply the word for water reduplicated. Water played an important part in religious ceremonies in old Hawai'i.

Fresh Water

As a people surrounded by the undrinkable ocean, fresh water was of prime importance. In wet areas of the islands, plenty was available for use. Streams were diverted to irrigate fields of *kalo* (taro), *'uala* (sweet potato), and other crops. After strenuous work or swimming in the sea, Hawaiians cleansed themselves with fresh water. Indeed, they often bathed five or more times a day.

Water from springs was preferred for drinking, as it was usually the purest. Fresh water was also used in food preparation and had its ritual applications as well.

In the dry areas of each island, fresh water was at a premium. It often had to be carried down from the mountains in huge gourds, or collected from rare springs. Fresh water springs were even found in the ocean. Divers would plunge into the ocean with covered water gourds, locate the springs, fill the gourds with fresh water, close them, and rise to the surface.

In arid areas, springs were considered to be sacred things. Springs that occasionally went dry were treated to lengthy rituals and given many offerings. Soon after these rites the springs would once again freely run. In some isolated places, water dripping from the ceilings of caves was collected in large wooden troughs and carefully poured into gourds. Such caves, used to collect drinking water, were sacred to Kane.

Blowholes, Kaua'i

Fresh water was important in the ritual purification of places and people, as during the dedication of a *heiau* or during treatment for sickness. Each day, the family altar (Pohaku-o-Kane) was sprinkled with water or coconut oil.

A magic spring, which existed on one of the sacred islands of the *akua,* was the source of the "water of life" or the "water of Kane." The water from this spring possessed great *mana,* for when sprinkled on a dead person it restored life. Many stories recount the exploits of humans who journeyed to this land, gathered some of the water, and used it to bring back their deceased friends or relatives.

Hawaiians usually mentioned the "Water of Life of Kane" when planting, harvesting, and offering fruits of their fields, because it was the source of life. Hawaiians were quite aware of the spiritual qualities of fresh water.

Rain

Uwe ka lani ola ka honua, runs the old chant: "The heavens cry, the earth lives." In this simple observation of the necessity of rain for bountiful crops lie many hidden meanings. In essence, it speaks of the primordial union of Papa and Wakea and of human sexuality. Water was seen to be so intimately connected with the generation of plant life that cool, fresh water was a common symbol of sexuality.

Since early Hawaiians were dependent upon the deities to provide them with water, they regularly prayed for rain. When a lack of rain created drought on an island, special temples were built or restored and Kane and Lono invoked to bring life-giving rains to the fields and to their worshippers.

Hawaiians used dozens of words to describe rain. Light, misty rain falling at certain times was considered to be a blessing from the *akua,* and a positive omen. Rainbows, though usually considered to be signs of the *ali'i* (they might appear above the heads of chiefs and chiefesses) or of good luck, could also be seen as omens of doom or treachery.

Meteorological *kahuna* spent much of their time watching the skies to predict the coming of rain or the ending of storms. There were many signs: red skies in the west at sunset indicated the rain would soon clear; blue-black clouds hugging the mountains were omens of rain, as were small clouds with red patches to the east before sunrise. Certain winds usually brought rain as well.

Salt Water

Though the ocean is usually associated with Kanaloa, Kane is also connected with the sea. According to Fornander, Kane added salt to the ocean's water to keep it healthy and uninfected.

The ocean provided an abundance of food stuffs, from seaweed to mollusks, crustaceans, and fish. The ancient Hawaiians also evaporated salt on the coasts of each island. Perhaps it was the ocean's role as a major provider of food, and its unquestioned power and vast size, that led to the many uses of sea water.

Samuel Manaiakalani Kamakau termed sea water the "universal remedy." When the digestion was poor, the patient drank two to four cups of sea water, followed this with a cup of fresh water, and then chewed sugar cane. This remedy acted as a laxative and soon restored normalcy.

Salt water also had ritual uses. A purification bath known as *kapu kai* was a ritual bath in the sea. It was performed in private and was accompanied with prayers. *Kapu kai* were necessary for all who had suffered any type of defilement (such as through contact with a corpse, after menstruation, and so on). The bath removed the *kapu* and the defiling *mana* from the person. Such baths were thought to be most effective if repeated for five consecutive days.

Additionally, these purification baths were used before a *hula* dancer's graduation from training, at the close of healing ceremonies, and at any time when a person felt the need.

Sea water (or salted water) was widely used for purification. A standard purification ritual was required before collecting offerings for

Diamond Head, Oahu

the *akua* or performing religious services. It consisted of washing or sprinkling the body with fresh water, followed by sprinkling with fresh water mixed with salt (or sea water), and then ablution with salt water mixed with *'olena* (turmeric root).

Most purifications simply used sea water, or fresh water mixed with salt. These were collected (or mixed) with prayer, for the waters themselves had little power without these prayers. At times the *kahuna* breathed onto the water to impart *mana* to the mixture before use, though anyone, *kahuna* or not, could mix and use purifying waters.

Such purificatory waters were generally known as *ka wai a kapu a Kane* ("the sacred waters of Kane"), or simply as *wai huikala* ("water of purification"). The process of using salt water for purification was known as *pi kai*. It was in almost constant use: for cleansing newborn babies, purifying new canoes and houses, creating *hula* altars to Laka, in the subincision ceremony of young boys, as part of healing rites, and after contact with defiling things. After menstruation each month women purified themselves with these waters, and objects inadvertently touched by menstruating women were similarly cleansed.

This ritual sprinkling of salt water is still performed throughout Hawai'i in both public and private settings to drive away evil and to purify homes, buildings, and construction sites. It's even often done, in a quasi-Christian framework, by Christian ministers, though the practice was in common use for centuries before the arrival of the first Western sailors and missionaries and has no direct connection with baptism.

The high regard that the Hawaiians had for saltwater was probably related to the fact that salt is a necessary part of the human diet. That, the fact that salt water doesn't turn bad, coupled with the obvious *mana* of the sea, probably led to its use in ritual and ceremony as a powerful purifier.

CHAPTER ELEVEN

Stone

Stones *(pohaku)* are possessors of *mana*. Some deities resided within stones, and images of *'aumakua* were carved from them. Ghosts could temporarily inhabit rocks and many humans were turned into stone by offended *akua*. As one of the most versatile materials available for use on volcanic islands, *pohaku* were revered.

Uses of *Pohaku*

The importance of stone to the Hawaiians can't be overstated. It was used to make sinkers for fishing lines, octopus lures, and nets; as anchors, *poi* pounders, hammers, axes, lamps (which held strings of oily nuts that were burned), and musical instruments for *hula*. Canoes and wooden objects were smoothed and polished with stone tools.

Weapons made of stone were deadly. Stones were hurled at enemies using slings or were thrown in battle. Special stones, which were grooved and secured with ropes, were thrown to sink enemy canoes during battles at sea, then retrieved via the rope to be used again. War clubs were fashioned of carefully worked stones attached to wooden handles.

Medicines were ground and prepared with stones, stones were used in the *imu* (underground oven) for cooking meats and vegetables, and hot stones were dropped into containers of water for cooking purposes. Piles of stones marked district boundaries and pathways. Stones were used in agriculture (to line *kalo* patches grown on dry land) and architecture (the creation of temples). They were also used by *kahuna* to teach the art of diagnosis.

Games played with stones included *kanone,* a form of checkers; *ulu maika,* similar to bowling in which round stones are rolled through obstacles; and the ancient game of skipping stones on calm waters known worldwide. Stones were also of importance in what we would term "magic" (i.e., the use of *mana* to produce astonishing results). Stones were also used by *kahuna* for divination.

This multitude of uses led to a saying: *He ola ka pohaku a he make ka pohaku* ("There is life in the stone and death in the stone").

Though limited to volcanic varieties, Hawaiians knew at least 54 varieties of stone. Each type possessed distinct *mana* which determined its proper uses. Prayer, offerings, and the inherent *mana* of their users enhanced the stone's power and intensified its effects.

Stones and the *Akua*

Though any stone could be the temporary resting spot for an *'aumakua* or could contain the *mana* of a goddess or god, some deities were specifically associated with stones. Kanepoha(ku)ka'a ("Rolling or Bursting, Cracking Stone Kane") was a god of stones. This *akua* was worshipped by warriors *(ko'a)* who asked him to make them as strong as stones, as well as by farmers. He appeared in the dreams of his worshippers as a human with a stone head, but no images of him were made.

A goddess worshipped locally in Ka-'u, Island of Hawai'i, was known as 'Ili'ili-hanau-o-Koloa ("birth pebble of Koloa"). She was the creatress of the porous stones found on the beach at Koloa, Hawai'i.

Few images of the *akua* were fashioned of stone, probably because lava is extremely hard and wood was much easier to manipulate with

The Queen's Bath, Big Island, Hawai'i

the limited number of tools then available. Unworked, naturally-shaped stones were sometimes used as images of the deities or *'aumakua*. The presence of these stones were often revealed to their worshippers in dreams.

Such images were generally rectangular in shape. A human-like face was often carved at one end, but other features were usually left uncarved. Families kept such *'aumakua* stones hidden and secretly worshipped at them. (Such stones are still safeguarded by a few old Hawaiian families today.)

Images of Ku'ula, god of fish and of fishing, were usually water-worn, elongated stone. Such stones could also be worked until they had a fish-like appearance. When cared for, these stones rewarded their caretakers with successful fishing. They preferred to be wrapped in *lipoa,* a type of seaweed.

Other "fishing" stones also existed. These contained a spirit that was placed in them by an *akua,* was invited in by humans through ritual and offerings, or who simply took up residence within the stone because it desired to do so. These stones weren't representations of Ku'ula. Fish-shaped stones were used for successful fishing and often were wrapped in *lipoa* seaweed. Such stones usually appeared in dreams to humans and chatted with them, and they often became quite attached to certain persons. Their locations were also usually revealed in dreams.

Though the relationship between these fish stones and humans was usually pleasant, if the stones became uncooperative or tiresome, the humans simply took them out to sea and dropped them over the side of the canoe, thus ending the relationship.

Birth Stones

O'ahu and Kaua'i possessed birthstones *(nohaku hanau)* to which chiefesses would go to give birth. This ensured that their children would be fully *ali'i* and would possess extra *mana* for having been born at such sites. These occasions were marked with great ceremony.

K'o, *a Hawaiian board game played with black and white stones*

If a common woman managed to give birth at such sacred stones, her offspring would be considered to be *ali'i*. This was rare, however, since the birthstones rested on *ali'i* compounds that were *kapu* to commoners. The birthstones on Kaua'i are at Holoholoku *heiau*, just above the Wailua river. On O'ahu they can be found at Kukaniloko, near Wahiawa. Other birth stones include the famous Naha stone (now located in front of the Kilo library on the island of Hawai'i, which a young Kamehameha once lifted) and a stone on the grounds of Punahou school on O'ahu.

The navel strings of babies were often wrapped and placed in crevices in stones and covered with tiny pebbles so that they wouldn't be eaten by rats. If this occurred, the child would grow up to be a thief.

Healing Stones

Stones with modern or ancient associations with healing are found throughout Hawai'i. One source states that they were usually located near the shoreline on each island, and that each of them was individually named.

On O'ahu, the Wahiawa Healing Stones are today housed in a small crypt-like structure at 108 California Street in Wahiawa, after having been moved several times. Though little is known of their early history, the stones were originally located at Kukaniloko, site of the birth stones mentioned above. During the 1920s through the outbreak of World War II, they gained a wonderful reputation as healers, and were visited by thousands of people. Offerings are still placed there on a regular basis.

The Wizard Stones near Waikiki beach are far less famous. They too have been moved a number of times. They now sit unobtrusively on Kuhio Beach (across the street from the Hyatt Regency Towers Hotel, about 100 feet from the Waikiki Police Station). These four stones are marked with a plaque describing their history.

The stones were imbued with healing *mana* by four Tahitian healer-magicians who visited Hawai'i in the 1500s, performed miraculous healings, then departed for their distant home. Before leaving, each moved healing *mana* into one stone. The stones are named after these wizards: Kapaemahu, Kahaloa, Kapuni, and Kinohi. (There is some doubt today as to whether these were four men, two men and two women, or some other combination.) These powerful stones, located in the heart of the tourist beach, are rarely visited today.

At Lahaina on Maui, a tilted, chair-shaped stone is often seen at low tide in the harbor. This stone, known as Hauola, was an ancient healing site. According to tradition, patients sat on the stone and allowed the salt water to wash over their bodies and, thus, to remove all illness.

Stones of Fertility

Many stones contained powerful fertility *mana*. Each island possessed at least one large phallic rock that assisted women with its *mana* to become pregnant. The majority of these stones have been destroyed, toppled, or otherwise forgotten.

The most famous fertility stone in Hawai'i today is Kauleonana-hoa (literally, "the penis of Nanahoa"). Located in Palaau State Park on the island of Moloka'i, Kauleonanahoa is a massive clump of lava six feet high, bearing a remarkable natural resemblance to the human penis. Legend states that it was once a man (Nanahoa) who was turned to stone for abusing his wife.

This Phallic Rock, as it's also known, was visited by infertile women who made offerings and spent prayerful nights at the base of the stone. By morning they were pregnant. The shapes of such rocks obviously revealed their special *mana*.

Near Kauleonanahoa lie two stone images, one female, one male. Whether these were artificially worked or not I've been unable to discover. Women apparently left offerings at these images before going to Kauleonanahoa.

The *mana* of such stones continues to be respected today, as is evidenced by the offerings still found at the base of Kauleonanahoa.

Most other phallic rocks have been forgotten or destroyed; only this one remains as a highly visible reminder of early Hawaiians' concerns for human fertility.

Even portable phallic rocks were apparently potent with fertility *mana*. Mary Kawena Pukui relates the story of a woman who found a banana-shaped rock washed up on the beach. She brought it home, left it in a trunk, and forgot about it. She soon had many babies. Upon finding the phallic *pohaku* in the trunk, her family gave it away. The woman's continuous births immediately halted. (These events took place in the twentieth century.)

Such phenomena weren't surprising to Hawaiians, for stones were understood to possess gender. Male stones include solid rock, *'a'a* lava (coarse and crumbly), and column-shaped or long stones (such as the banana shaped *pohaku* previously mentioned). Female stones include porous rocks, *pahoehoe* (smooth-flowing) lava, loaf-shaped or round stones, and rocks split with hollows.

Certain types of stones were known to give birth. The finest of these were found at Punalu'u, Ka-'u District, Island of Hawai'i. Female stones of this type are quite porous, covered with small holes. Male stones lack these holes and so are smooth.

Placing a male stone with a female stone and keeping them either wrapped in *kapa* (bark cloth) or under water will result in the birth of pebbles, which might grow to become large rocks. These were then used, after proper ceremonies, as figures of the *akua*.

Pohaku, then, were sacred to the Hawaiians. They were used to induce pregnancy, to bless births, to grow and prepare food, to create temples, to heal, to secure good fishing, to divine the future, to pass the time, to win during battle, and for a host of other uses.

The *mana* contained within *pohaku*, as indicated by their many uses, was such that they became central to life in old Hawai'i.

CHAPTER TWELVE

Color

Hawai'i is a land of contrasting colors. Both above and below the surface of the ocean, an incredible variety of hues assaults the eye. Keenly observant of nature, Hawaiians used colors garnered from it to separate commoners from chiefs, as offerings to the deities, and in both spiritual and physical remedies.

Color was one of the ways in which Hawaiians classified the natural world around them. Their method of categorizing plants, animals, stones, fish, and other objects by their colors, markings, and shapes led to a sophisticated system of natural science. Much of this observation was used for religious purposes.

Four colors played predominant roles in the spiritual and physical lives of early Hawaiians.

Red ('Ula, 'Ula'ula)

The color of freshly shed blood, of hot lava and *'ohi'a lehua* blooms and wood, red was a color of sanctity. The Hawaiians apparently received reverence for this color from their original island homes, for red is the predominantly sacred color throughout Polynesia.

Dedicated to Ku, especially in his Ku'ula aspect, red was also sacred to Lono: redfish were offered to him. The unique images of Kuka'ilimoku, Kamehameha I's war god, were decorated with red feathers. Temporary Lono temples built to ensure rain and abundance of crops were stained red by the use of a native plant. Red was also used in ritual objects. Red bark cloth (known as *ha'ena*) was used to wrap or to "clothe" images of the deities, particularly Ku.

Red was a color sacred to Pele. When deceased family members were to be transfigured into *'aumakua*, they were wrapped in red (or red and black) bark cloth and offered to the goddess in hot lava.

Ka-moho-ali'i, the shark brother of Pele, sometimes appeared in human form. As a man he was always seen wearing a red *malo* (loincloth). Thus, red wasn't worn on the beach by those who respected Ka-moho-ali'i.

What was fit for the gods was also fit for their earthly relatives, the *ali'i*. Thus, red was one of the favored colors for the spectacular ceremonial regalia with which the chiefs decorated themselves. Feather capes, helmets, and even loincloths were made of a fiber netting covered with thousands of red feathers gathered from the *'i'iwi* (a now endangered native honeycreeper) and other birds.

Why was red such a sacred color? Perhaps because of its associations with blood and childbirth, or because much of the land in Hawai'i is bright red, thanks to its recent volcanic origin. Red was also seen in berries of the *'ohelo* and the flowers and wood of the *'ohi'a lehua*, two plants that grow on lava flows. Hawai'i's sunrises and sunsets may have also been partially responsible for the reverence of red.

Black *('Ele'ele)*

This is another color owned by Lono, possibly because the rich volcanic earth from which Lono's bounty springs is often black. Black rain clouds were also sacred to this god.

Black pigs were among those things that were offered to Lono. In building *mapele* (abundance) temples to Lono, wood from the *lama* tree was preferred. This wood has a black bark which, as the color of Lono, was ideally suited to promote fertility of the fields.

A form of Kane, Kane-hekili (worshipped as an *'aumakua*) was seen, when he appeared in dreams, as a man, one side of his body black, the other white; feet on the earth, head touching the clouds. His priests dressed in black and offered him their dead wrapped in black.

There appears to have been no negative associations with black. This color was intimately connected with the natural phenomena that were the *akua*. Black lava, black storm clouds, and the blackness of night *(po)* were seen as natural aspects of life, and contained no negative, dangerous, or evil qualities.

White *(Kea)*

As in many other parts of the world, white was a sacred color. *Kahuna pule* (prayer experts) usually wore white *malo* and shoulder cloaks while performing rituals in the temples. The prayer or oracle towers of the temples were covered with white *kapa*. Bark cloth of this color was also used in making the symbol of Lono, the Lonomakua, centerpiece of the yearly Makahiki festival.

During family purification rites, *ninikea* (white *kapa*) were used. Additionally, fine white *kapa* of the *'oloa* type were used to cover or to gird images of the *akua*.

The reverence for this color isn't difficult to understand. White is seen in ocean waves, the clouds, and in flowers. The absence of other discernible colors seems to indicate purity. Additionally, Hawaiians also knew white snow: the snow goddess of Mauna Kea, Poliahu, wears a white cloak (the snow).

Yellow *(Melemele)*

This is another sacred color of the *ali'i,* and was probably of more importance than red in this context. Feather *lei* (worn only by women), capes, helmets, and images of the deities were often made of yellow feathers, usually interspersed with more common red feathers. Yellow was also *kapu* to some fishing deities.

This color also had its religious uses. Yellow *kapa* was offered to Kane; in fact, this seems to have been his favorite color. The altar of the *hula* goddess, Laka, was always adorned with a block of *lama* wood, wrapped with bark cloth dyed with *'olena* (turmeric) to a nice shade of yellow. The use of *'olena* in creating purification waters probably originated from both its color and scent.

Relatives of *mo'o* (lizard *'aumakua)* and water spirits wrapped the bodies of their deceased relatives in yellow during the rite *(kaku'ai)* that transfigured them into new *'aumakua.* Images of the great *mo'o* goddess popularized by Kamehameha, Kihawahine, were also wrapped with yellow bark cloth.

The brilliantly yellow thigh feathers of the *'o'o* or *'o'o 'a'a* bird were used in making feather garments for the *ali'i.* Yellow feathers were also gathered from the *mamo* bird. (These birds are apparently extinct today, thanks to predators introduced by Westerners to Hawai'i. Hawaiians usually didn't kill birds for their feathers; they caught them using sticky gums, removed the few needed feathers, and released them into the wild.)

Many other colors had spiritual significance in old Hawai'i. These are just a few of the hues that helped to shape the Hawaiians' religious practices and their lives.

CHAPTER THIRTEEN

Plants

Centuries before immigrants brought exotic flowers from China, India, Japan, tropical America, Europe, and elsewhere, the Polynesian voyagers who settled Hawai'i introduced useful plants to the local landscape. These included bananas, sweet potatoes, sugar, breadfruit, gourds, arrowroot, and others. These were necessary for food, medicine, ornament, magic, and religious ritual.

They also found uses for many of the plants that grew in Hawai'i before the arrival of others. Hundreds of plants were named and their specific applications were passed to each generation.

Hawaiians realized that plants were more than physical objects. Many plants were the bodies of specific deities, and so were sacred to those that worshipped these *akua*. Others were bodies of *'aumakua;* thus, they were relatives. Still others possessed great *mana* (spiritual power) and with them wonders (magic, or *ho'okalakupua*) could be performed.

Rituals were performed during planting and harvesting, when gathering medicinal herbs, and when using plants in many ways. Stone was difficult to work, large planks of wood were rare, and metal and pottery were unknown. Plants were therefore used to create a variety of objects, including clothing, shelter, mats, pillows, furniture, weapons, tools, sports equipment, soap, musical instruments, rope and cord, and even knives. Plants provided artificial light, travel (canoes), perfumery materials, flavorings, tattoo dyes, and temporary body decoration.

Plants played important roles in ritual. Images of the deities were often made of plant materials. Temples were usually graced with certain types of plants. Plants were offered to the *akua* and often formed part of the altar itself. Many types of plants were used in protection, divination, purification, love attraction or repulsion, cursing, and other magical practices. These plants were chosen for such uses due to their potent *mana*.

The most important use of plants was, of course, as a source of nourishment. Food was so revered and necessary that war was forbidden during planting and harvesting—an extraordinarily humane concept and the antithesis of the Western combat strategy of starving out the enemy. Even battle wasn't allowed to interfere with food production.

Some plants were cultivated. Others were gathered from the forests, valleys, plains, lava flows, and the ocean. When crops failed during infrequent droughts, many native plants were used as famine food. Today, perhaps the most celebrated manner in which Hawaiians use flowers and plants is the *lei*.

Lei

It's impossible to say who made the first *lei*. Surely before migrating from Tahiti the people later known as Hawaiians made wreaths of various objects in their homelands, and brought the custom to Hawai'i. Wreaths, crowns, and necklaces of flowers are known worldwide, and have been in use as long as humans have felt the need or desire to decorate their bodies.

Lei were made and used for a number of reasons in old Hawai'i, and not all were worn. Some were purely decorative; others had spiritual significance. Certain types were reserved for the chiefly class, and a very few could only be worn by women.

In Hawai'i, both temporary and permanent *lei* were made. Permanent *lei* were fashioned of a variety of materials: feathers (reserved for female chiefs), land and sea shells, seeds, nuts, and ringlets of braided human hair. Temporary *lei* were made of ferns, flowers, fruits, seaweed and other native and introduced plant materials.

Lei of both types were used for sacred purposes. In common with most other pleasing aspects of human life, the deities enjoyed the fine art of making, wearing, and giving away these floral garlands.

Lei created for and worn during *hula* were especially sacred, since the garland remained the property of the goddess Laka (though it might have been worn by humans). Such *lei* were carefully handled. Placing an "ordinary" *lei* on top of one dedicated to Laka was forbidden. *Lei* were also left at temples as offerings, or were worn during religious rites.

Some beliefs concerning *lei* have been preserved. Pregnant women were warned against wearing *lei* because the child might be strangled with its umbilical cord. Giving away a *lei* that had been presented to

*Plumeria blossoms, a favorite of the author,
held by David Harrington*

you was considered most unfortunate. Additionally, it was considered wrong to ask for a *lei* that another was wearing.

Carelessly leaving a *lei* one had worn where others could find it, or giving it to some unknown person, was both foolish and dangerous, for the *lei* contained some of its wearer's *mana*. This made it ideal for use in sorcerous magic against the original wearer. Dreaming of a *lei* usually indicated that someone known to the dreamer was pregnant.

The contemporary practice of presenting a *lei* with a kiss isn't ancient, for Hawaiians didn't kiss, not even on the cheek. Their usual form of affectionate greeting was to place the nose beside that of the one being greeted. The "ancient" custom known today probably originated in the 1930s.

Though some persons still consider the *lei* to be spiritual or even magical, these floral wreaths have lost much of their magic. Even the materials used in their construction have changed.

The variety of flowers and leaves used in *lei* made today wouldn't be recognized by old Hawaiians. Plumeria, carnations (orchids), pikake, white ginger, and roses were then unknown. Lacking these materials, early Hawaiians twisted native ferns into anklets, bracelets, and crowns; threaded seeds or berries; entwined fragrant vines; or strung the few available flowers. The introduction of foreign plants to Hawai'i has widened the options of all *lei* makers.

Though this chapter is rather lengthy, just a few of the most important plants used in old Hawai'i are discussed here. Where possible, I've included the Hawaiian name, common English name, and the plant's specific Latin name. Some plants have no English equivalents. (Note: For more information, see Deneger, Handy and Handy, Krauss, MacDonald, and Neal in the Bibliography.)

'Awa

The 'awa (Piner methysticum) is traditionally believed to have originated in Kahiki by the deities for their enjoyment as well as that of humans. It was one of the most sacred of plants, and was offered to virtually every akua (particularly Kane and Kanaloa), as well as to the 'aumakua (especially shark ancestors). 'Awa is known elsewhere in Polynesia as kava or kava-kava.

This plant was considered to be sacred because its roots were used to produce a potent narcotic drink. The drink soothed the commoners who had worked all day, stifled angry emotions, brought sleep, and assisted kahuna in predicting the future. It was also drunk for pleasure. (Since it has a bitter, woody taste, sweet foods were usually eaten after drinking the liquid.)

The root was prepared by chewing until it was reduced to a finely minced mass. This was squeezed and strained through a temporary net-like object and the potent juice poured into cups made from coconut shells.

In small doses, 'awa refreshes the senses and eases tensions. Larger amounts inhibit movement and cause sleep. 'Awa affects the central nervous system (just as does alcohol, though 'awa isn't alcoholic). Curiously, though, 'awa intoxication doesn't induce violence, as does intoxication with alcohol. A person drunk on 'awa is incapable of fighting.

A drink with such wondrous properties, so beloved by humans, was also enjoyed by the deities. It was offered to them to soothe their tempers, to feed their souls, and to assist in asking for favors. It was considered to be as necessary for the nourishment of the akua as fish and poi were to humans. Offerings of 'awa were usually made by pouring or sprinkling the liquid over an image of the akua. In the absence of such religious images, it was sprinkled on the ground. Both the prepared beverage and the roots of the plant were popular offerings.

Everyone drank 'awa, though some varieties, known by their color and markings, were reserved for the ali'i (chiefs).

Its ritual uses were many. It was used in the consecration of young boys, the dedication of new *hula* dancers, in healing rituals, and in rites of divination and possession.

'Awa's ritual properties were enhanced by its medicinal powers. It was drunk to lose weight and used to treat asthma, urinary tract problems, and rheumatism. Many varieties of 'awa can still be found growing wild throughout Hawai'i.

Hala

The *hala (Pandanus odoratissimus)* is a member of the screwpine family, many species of which are grown in tropical zones around the world. In Hawai'i, it usually grows near the ocean at low elevations.

For centuries, the leaves of the *hala* were used in thatching houses. Its stiff, strong leaves *(lauhala)* were useful for making mats, fans, baskets, pillows, and what would today be termed "tackle boxes"—baskets to hold fishing lines and hooks.

Lei were sometimes made of the fruit, which resembles a pineapple and separates into finger-shaped sections known as "keys." *Lei* made of these yellow to orange keys were beautiful and possessed a delicious fragrance. However, they were seldom worn because they were thought to be unlucky.

This idea probably arose from a sacred story: Hi'iaka, sister of Pele, was wearing a *lei hala* when a *kahuna* asked her to assist in saving a gravely ill patient. Hi'iaka said that it was too late, for the patient was already gone *(hala)*. Additionally, Kapo, the sorcery goddess, wore a *lei hala* so often that it became one of her symbols, and so was deemed unfortunate. To this day, wearing the *lei hala* is considered to be unfortunate on any day but New Year's Day. To present one to a candidate running for office is sure to mean her or his defeat. However, *lei hala* are given and worn to mark the completion of important tasks (such as graduation), and are also worn so that misfortunes will slip away.

These *lei* were regarded as being so negative that a fishermen going to the sea would, upon meeting a person wearing a *lei hala,* return home. No fish would be caught that day.

The pungent aroma of the flowers were used by women in love magic and as perfume. The fragrance was considered to be aphrodisiac in effect upon those men who smelled it, and so both the flowers and their pollen were collected and used for this purpose.

The dried, separated fruits were used as paintbrushes. They were also placed into containers of water to create a different type of "water of purification."

Hala doesn't seem to have been a *kino lau* of any *akua*.

'Ilima

'Ilima (Sida fallax) is a small shrub that is found throughout the islands at low elevations. It delights in growing on otherwise bare cliffs near the ocean.

This plant became famed throughout Hawai'i because of its small yellow, orange, or red five-petaled flowers. The plant is sacred to Laka (goddess of the *hula),* Ka'ahupahau (shark goddess of Pearl Harbor), and to Kane 'Apua, a younger brother of Pele who was a healer and a god of *taro* planters. The plant is one of the forms that Laka and Kane 'Apua could assume.

Lei of these flowers were quite popular, even though hundreds of blossoms were required to make each *lei,* and the flowers wilt a day after being picked. The orange crepe paper *lei* that were so popular 50 or so years ago were made in imitation of the feathery *lei 'ilima*.

A common untruth about old Hawai'i is that only the *ali'i* could wear the *lei 'ilima*. Mary Kawena Pukui states that this is an error, as the *lei* could by made and worn by anyone, though its creation was time-consuming. Some considered the *lei 'ilima* to be unfortunate to wear. It was thought to attract mischievous spirits if worn, but many found this beautiful, fragile *lei* quite delightful.

Planting of the *'ilima* (which ensured the necessary steady supply of the flowers) was done in an unique manner: a limpet shell was placed upside-down in a hole in the ground, and the *'ilima* shoot placed within it. All was then buried. This was done to give the new plant the firmness of the *'onihi,* which holds fast to wave-splashed rocks.

Medicinally, juice of the *'ilima* was given to children as a mild laxative, and pregnant women ate its blossom as a part of prenatal care.

Magically, the flowers were used to determine if love was strong. (See Chapter 19.)

Ipu (Gourd)

Gourds were one of the many bodies *(kino lau)* of Lono, god of agriculture. According to some sacred stories, the world and everything in it was created from a gourd. Lono was the cosmic gourd that brought rain from the sky-gourd to make the gourds grow.

Planting and tending gourds involved much ritual and prayer to this deity. While growing in the field, they were carefully guarded. As bodies of Lono, they couldn't be planted where the shadows of persons walking by would fall on them.

Once collected, the gourds were processed and made into useable objects. (Bitter gourds were used only for medicine.) Gourds were necessary for carrying food, fish, and water from place to place. *Ipu* were hung from the rafters and used to store clothing, feather garments, *lei*, and salt in the home. Gourds were also used for *hula* drums and as tools of divination. They were placed in burial caves and shrines. One expert states that the Hawaiians had 36 different uses for gourds.

Gourds were so highly prized that they weren't even safe while not yet ripe. A thief might steal a prize specimen nearly ready for picking. To avoid this, the prudent farmer named each growing gourd after an ancestor *('aumakua)*. This prevented theft: the fruits were under the protection of these *'aumakua*.

Kalo (Tahitian: *Taro*)

The *kalo (Colocasia* spp.) was the main vegetable food source for the Hawaiians. All Hawaiians are descended from the first *kalo*. Wakea and Papa (or, as it is usually recounted, Papa's daughter, Ho'o-hoku-kalani), had a son. This son was born as a deformed child (or a root) that was buried in the ground. It sprouted as the first *kalo* plant. The couple had another child, a normal human son, named Haloa, and a third, also named Haloa. The first Haloa became a *kalo* plant, while the second became the ancestor of all the Hawaiian people. Because of this lineage, all humans are descended from the *kalo*.

There are many stories concerning *kalo*. One tells of two beautiful *kalo* that loved each other. A chief decided to serve them up in a feast; so, to preserve their lives, they moved to another part of the patch. The vegetables repeatedly moved until they could no longer hide from the chief who greatly desired to eat them. The two *kalo* finally "took wing" and flew from patch to patch. Eventually, a kind man graciously hid them in his patch, where the two *kalo* happily lived out their years together.

Kalo was sacred to Kane, and was used in offerings to many other *akua*.

Poi, one of the most important of ancient Hawai'i's foodstuffs, was made from *kalo*. *Poi* was the bread of the Hawaiians; the staff of life. It was eaten at each meal with relish; sometimes alone, at other times to flavor certain foods. *Poi* was sacred. When the bowl was uncovered (ready for eating), there could be no arguing, scolding, or discussion of serious business.

Early Hawaiian farmers developed countless varieties of *kalo*—perhaps as many as 300. Most of them are now long gone, but in old Hawai'i various types of *kalo* could be used as replacement offerings to many *akua* if the preferred items weren't available. When a specific type of fish was needed for blessing a new house's main post, a certain type of *kalo* could be substituted. If a family was too poor to offer a pig in sacrifice, a dark *kalo* was just as suitable. Many such substitutions were made from the varieties of *kalo* that were then available.

The tender young leaves of the *kalo* were also eaten in a variety of dishes, including one with coconut milk and octopus, *lu'au*. The name of this dish became synonymous with that of the popular, modern Hawaiian feast-party. (The old Hawaiian name was *'aha'aina*.)

Ki

The *ki* (*Dracaena terminalis;* more commonly known today as *ti,* pronounced "tee"), was one of the most useful plants in old Hawai'i. Its long, broad leaves were used to make temporary rain capes (worn while travelling in the rainy mountains), sandals, whistles, food containers, insect whisks, and food wrappers. They served as plates and cups. *Ki* was also used in thatching structures in peaceful temples, for thatching houses, and as a container for transporting flower *lei.* The root was eaten as a famine food and as a delicacy (when baked); the plant also had medicinal applications. *Ki* was among the altar decorations of Laka.

Its most famous uses were in the arena of magic and ritual. These uses have been so well remembered that today, tourists are offered *"Ti, the Hawaiian Good Luck Plant"* in hundreds of gift shops throughout the islands. Though the magical and ritual uses of other plants have largely been forgotten, it's rare to see a traditional Hawaiian home that doesn't have *ki* planted nearby.

Ki *as Protection*

Ki were consummate protectors. *Ki* was planted around dwellings to safeguard the houses and the family against all manner of dangers. (An ancient Hawaiian "house" consisted of a series of unattached structures.) *Ki* were also planted near *kalo* plants to guard these vital sources of food.

Humans protected themselves by wearing *ki* leaves around the waist, the ankles, or around the neck. A leaf was slipped inside clothing. Sleeping persons were guarded by placing *ki* leaves under the sleeping mats.

If a menstruating woman had to cross Pele's home, she wore bracelets, anklets, and a *lei* of *ki* leaves, and was accompanied on either side by a man bearing a stalk of the same plant. This was done for protection against Pele's wrath at being so disturbed by the woman's strong *mana.*

Food that had to be moved about at night was protected from hungry ghosts by wrapping it in *ki* leaves. Sailors were safeguarded from severe storms and drowning by the presence of a *ki* leaf somewhere in the canoe. A *ki* leaf attached to canoes also provided good fishing.

A unique use of *ki* determined whether specific rivers near the sea, which were inhabited by sharks, were safe to cross. A stalk of *ki* was throw into the water. If it quickly disappeared, the shark was present; it was unsafe to cross. If it stayed afloat, it was safe to swim across the river. A similar ritual was used to determine whether specific beaches were shark-free.

Ki *in Exorcism*

Ki was also used as a tool of exorcising places or persons. In purifying a place, the *kahuna pule* (prayer expert) mixed fresh water, salt, and perhaps turmeric. This liquid was sprinkled around the premises with a *ki* leaf to drive away spirits.

Personal exorcisms were usually a part of healing. The aim of such rituals was to remove the evil spirit that had created the patient's illness. During these rites, the *kahuna* might lightly strike the possessed with *ki* leaves. If a child needed exorcising, *ki* leaves would be placed in a cup of salt water, which the child would then drink. The patient was often laid on a bed of *ki* leaves during these and other exorcisms.

Ki *in Healing*

Ki had many medicinal applications. It was usually used in treating simple ailments: a leaf was rubbed or placed on the stomach to ease the pain of a stomachache, or was placed against the stomach to relieve sea sickness while voyaging. A single *ki* leaf was dipped in cool water and tied around the head to relieve headache and fever. The instant each leaf became warm to the touch, it was replaced with a cool one.

Ki *leaf blessing on a* heiau

Ki was also internally used: a tightly furled new leaf was chewed to treat dry coughs. When eaten to excess, it was laxative in effect.

Other Uses

Aside from those mentioned above, *ki* had many other uses. *Kahuna pule* often carried or wore a *ki* leaf as a symbol of power and authority (and to utilize the *mana* contained within it). This was common on ceremonial occasions.

A stalk of the plant, held aloft in battle, was a sign of truce. Interwoven *ki* leaves formed the base for the cup of *'awa* during mediumistic rites, and *lei ki* were left at fishing shrines.

A *ki* leaf tied around the tail of the *'onelu* fish prevented those that ate it from developing a rash associated with eating this fish. When a tree was transplanted, a *ki* leaf was placed in the hole that the tree had once occupied.

Uses of Ki *Today*

Many of the ancient uses of *ki* are still being practiced. Men and women wear *ki* for protection, and plant it profusely around their homes (for both decoration and protection). *Ki* leaves are placed in some Honolulu high-rise buildings' elevators to guard their occupants; this is especially done to guard women against rape. Many fishing boats still bear a *ki* leaf for fishing luck. The ritual sprinkling of water with a *ki* leaf is still used when homes are disturbed or when ground is being broken for a new building. While hiking in the damp mountains, a shredded *ki* leaf is one of the most effective insect swatters.

Evidence of the most visible contemporary use of *ki* leaves can be seen at sacred sites throughout the islands. Rocks, fruits, and flowers are carefully wrapped in *ki* leaves and left as offerings to the deities at temples. Such offerings are often made for healings and are the modern alternative of the ancient food offerings once made in these same places (though food is also offered).

One seemingly modern use of *ki* in magic utilizes its protective *mana*. It is in use in at least one family on the Island of Kaua'i, where my informant was born and raised. The ritual consists of cutting a square out of a large *ki* leaf, placing *alae* (red earth) salt onto the leaf, rolling it into a cylinder, and placing it secretly within the house to guard it. If placed beneath or near the door it will prevent those with negative *mana* from crossing the threshold. (Unfortunately, I wasn't able to record any words used to accompany this rite.)

This simple, beautiful plant still holds a fascination for the people of Hawai'i.

(It should be noted that this multitude of uses pertain only to the original green *ki*. The red and variegated varieties were only lately introduced to Hawai'i, and have no traditional ritual Hawaiian uses.)

Ko (Sugar Cane)

Ko (*Saccharum* spp.) was probably brought to Hawai'i during the migration period. It was identified with Kane and was widely employed as a food, a medicine, and a tool of magic. (For sugar as a love-inducer see Chapter 17.)

Early Hawaiians knew many variety of *ko*, perhaps 40 or so. Each had specific uses. At least two varieties of *ko* were administered as general medicinal tonics, but sugar cane's main healing use seems to have been sweetening the mouth after taking foul-tasting herbal remedies. (Sometimes juice extracted from roasted stalks of *ko* was added to the remedies themselves.) One variety is said to have been used as a medicine during childbirth. Yet another type was offered to shark *'aumakua* as a substitute for the *lele* variety of banana.

Sugar was also enjoyed as a food or condiment. It was eaten as a snack between meals and was a favorite of children. During times of famine or on long journeys undertaken with little food, chewing *ko* satisfied hunger and sustained life.

The tassels and stalks of the sugar cane were used by children in a game that resembled darts, and houses were sometimes thatched with the leaves.

Unprocessed, fresh sugar cane is quite refreshing when chewed or sucked. Its juice is sweet, but not overpoweringly so like processed sugar. It also possesses a slight brown-sugar taste unlike sugar in any other form.

Kukui

The *kukui (Aleurites moluccana),* also known as the candlenut, is a large, handsome tree bearing light green foliage and hard nuts. The tree was probably brought to Hawai'i by its first inhabitants. This tree was a *kino lau* of Kamapua'a, who is in himself a form of Lono. It was of great value.

The oily nuts were chewed and spat onto the surface of the sea, to allow fishermen to more clearly see their prey. The plant produced many dyes, including a fine black dye used for tattooing, and the gum that exudes from the bruised bark was used by birdcatchers.

To make a lamp, prepared *kukui* nut kernels were strung on a piece of the midrib of a coconut leaf and placed in a carved stone cup.

The top nut was lit and the lamp shone for two to three minutes, at which time the spent kernel was knocked off and the next lit. Other lamps consisted of the same stone base filled with expressed *kukui* oil and ignited by means of a wick made from a strip of twisted *kapa*. Torches for outdoor gatherings were also made of *kukui*.

The nuts were roasted, mixed with salt, and eaten as a garnish known as *'inamona*. Consumed to excess, *kukui* nuts are a powerful purgative, and so they never played an important role in the everyday diet. The *kukui* had magical uses as well. During a ceremony to punish a thief, a fire was ritually kindled through friction and three *kukui* nuts were broken. The *kahuna* threw one of the kernels into the fire while praying that the thief would die. If the thief made himself or herself known to the *kahuna*, restitution was made. If not, the two remaining kernels were burned and it was certain that the thief would die. Today, the shells of the *kukui* are fashioned into beautiful jewelry as they were in antiquity. Various types of *lei kukui* were greatly appreciated.

Lama

Lama (*Diospyros* spp.), a relative of ebony, is a hardwood that grows in the forests of Hawai'i. It was a block of this wood, wrapped with yellow bark cloth, that represented the *hula* goddess Laka on her altar. The word *lama* means "light." The wood was used in the construction of the structures within peaceful temples. Additionally, a small structure was often built of *lama* wood during a single day while the sun shone. It was created and used for rituals to heal the sick. The houses of the *ali'i* that were surrounded by a fence of *lama* were *kapu* to all but a few persons. To enter such a place was to risk death.

Limu

Many seaweeds *(limu)* were valued as sources of food and medicine. Some had specific ritual uses. Though much of this information has been lost, some fragments have been recorded.

The *limu palahalaha (Ulva fasciata;* green sea lettuce) was used in *lei* by *hula* dancers. Conversely, eating another type of seaweed, the *limu line'ene'e (Laurencia* spp.) was forbidden to dancers, for part of the seaweed's name *(ne'ene'e)* means "hidden" or "clandestine." Eating this seaweed would cause the secrets of the dance to be hidden from its dancers.

Limu Kala

The *limu kala (Sargassum echinocarpum)* is a common seaweed, distinguished from other types by its toothed leaves that resemble those of the holly plant.

This seaweed's name *(kala*—"to forgive") reveals its usage. To assist a patient to recover from physical, emotional, and/or spiritual ills, the *kahuna la'au lapa'au* (herbal expert) would fashion an open-ended *lei* of freshly-gathered *limu kala.* Short strands of the seaweed were tied together to make a beautiful open-ended *lei.* This *lei* was placed around the patient's neck. The patient was then instructed to walk into the sea.

Black sand beach, Big Island, Hawai'i

The waves would crash against the patient. Soon she or he would be swimming. The sea would wash away the seaweed *lei,* loosening *(kala)* and removing the sickness.

Limu kala was also used in other ways in ritual. The seaweed was added to the *wai huikala* ("water of purification") which was sprinkled by the *kahuna pule* on mourners after the death and burial of a beloved. Washed in fresh water, it was ceremonially eaten after the *ho'oponopono* (a prayerful family ceremony designed to set right its affairs through prayer, discussion, confession, and forgiveness. Abbott (see Bibliography) states that this is the reason why the seaweed received the name *kala).*

Lei limu kala are still offered at fishing shrines by those who work the waters or by anyone grateful for the sea's gifts. I've also seen *lei limu kala* draped around upright stones on temples throughout the islands, even those in the mountains.

Medicinally, this seaweed was chopped and placed as a poultice on open cuts caused by razor sharp coral.

Mai'a (Banana)

Bananas are a *kino lau* of Kanaloa, and both he and his friend Kane were famous banana growers. This pair of gods brought the banana to Hawai'i from Kahiki. By the time foreigners arrived, about 70 varieties were growing in Hawai'i.

Many types of bananas were offered to the deities. At least one variety of banana *(Musa* spp.), the *mai'a lele,* was especially favored for this purpose. Its fruit was placed on the offering stand so that its essence would "fly" to the *akua,* but was never planted near homes because it would cause their occupants to fly elsewhere (*lele* means "to fly" or "flying"). This same type of tall banana tree was often planted to shelter a temple's altar. *Mai'a lele* were also used in love magic to make love "fly" to the victim. Another variety of banana was fed to shark *'aumakua* by fishermen of the Ka-'u district of the island of Hawai'i.

Nearly every type of banana was *kapu* to women. They could eat only the *mai'a iho lena* and *mai'a popo'ula* types without risking death for breaking a food *kapu*. This may not have been much of a hardship, as bananas seem to have been considered a delicacy rather than a staple in the Hawaiian diet. Some say that only the *ali'i* and *kahuna pule* ate them. Still, in time of famine, they were readily eaten by all.

A truly magical use of bananas has been recorded: They were used as a magical protectant. Hawaiians accepted the fact that *'aumakua* could occasionally have sex with living persons during the night. These spirit mates *(wahine o ka po* or *kane o ka po*—woman mate of the night or man mate of the night) sometimes caused no harm or problems to their living spouses, and could be of help: one couple had never had children. The woman began dreaming that a man who perfectly resembled her husband came to her from the sea. After each such dream she became pregnant.

Unfortunately, such relationships could be dangerous. Men and women who enjoyed the nighttime embraces of spirit lovers could become so enthralled with their spectral spouses that they stopped eating, sickened, and died. Alternately, the *kane* or *wahine o ka po* could coax the living partner to die and join him or her in the spirit world.

To prevent this from occurring, the flower sheath of a banana plant was laid between the legs near the thighs. This effectively ended the relationship by halting the spirit lover's nocturnal visits.

Hawaiians had a complex relationship with *mai'a*. They certainly ate them (often baked), but seem to have been concerned about the fruit's appearance. They're never mentioned in *mele* (songs), but were often used in derogatory sayings when describing others.

Fishermen wouldn't allow bananas on board their canoes, perhaps because they resemble eels, or because the slippery fruits would make the fish slip off their hooks. Meeting a person carrying them was considered unfortunate, and even dreaming of bananas was dangerous.

Hula dancers also shared a dislike of the fruit, believing that eating it, or even its presence, would cause the dancer's knowledge to "slip away."

The planting of bananas was strictly controlled, as they were bodies of the *akua*. The plants were best planted exactly at astronomical noon; i. e., when the sun stood directly overhead and cast no shadows. This would make the tree grow quickly to maturity, as the sun's *mana* would travel directly into the trunk.

In planting *keiki* (baby) banana plants, the farmer dug a deep hole, ate until he was quite full, then took off his *malo* (loin cloth), recited a prayer, and planted the young plant.

All empty holes were seen as omens of death. To avert the danger, a banana, part of the stalk of the plant, or a baby banana plant was placed in the hole and immediately filled in.

Certain types of *mai'a* were used in medicine. Juice of the roots of some varieties was given to babies to treat thrush.

Maile

Maile (Alyxia olivaeformis) was found in many forms in Hawai'i, and four of these were thought to be sisters. The glossy green vine was sacred to Laka, goddess of *hula*, and decorated her altars.

This plant has always been used in making open-ended *lei*. Once, this *lei* had another use. Opposing chiefs who decided (or were forced by *kapu)* to end a battle would meet at a temple and together weave a *lei* of *maile*. This *lei* marked the end of fighting, and the news was quickly spread to the warriors.

Upon drying, *maile* develops a sweet fragrance, and so was often kept in *ipu* (gourd containers) to scent clothing made of bark cloth. *Maile* was also an offering to the *akua* at temples.

Niu (Coconut)

Coconut trees aren't prolific in Hawai'i, and never seem to have been as common there as on South Pacific islands (Hawai'i is actually in the North Pacific). However, they were "among those things worshipped on Earth" as they were intimately related to Ku—*niu (Cocos nucifera)* was one of his bodies. As such, it was *kapu* for women to eat coconuts.

Rudely cutting down all coconut trees in a district was a declaration of war (perhaps because the trees were bodies of Ku, and one of his manifestations is as a war *akua).*

Coconut trees, which may reach heights of 100 feet in Hawai'i, are involved in many sacred stories, and water from a coconut was sometimes used by *kahuna kilo* in divination.

Niu was usually planted with an octopus. The octopus was placed in the bottom of the hole, and the tree on top of it. The long-tentacled octopus would increase the height of the tree. (It probably also served as a good fertilizer.) When a *niu* refused to bear coconuts, a pregnant woman might embrace the tree's trunk to stimulate its fertility.

The trees were quite useful. The swelling base of the tree was used to make large bowls and drums (which were covered with stretched shark skin). The fruits were fashioned into small drums for use in *hula*, and cups *('apu)* for drinking *'awa* and medicines. Oil was extracted and used to anoint the body and hair. The fibers were plaited

Waimea Canyon from helicopter, Kaua'i

to make rope. The leaves were woven into fans and balls, which were a favorite children's toy. Many medicines were made with coconut water, the flesh, and the shell.

'Ohelo

The *'ohelo (Vaccinium reticulatum)* has long been sacred to Pele. It grows wild on the Big Island, particularly on old lava flows, and bears scarlet berries. The plant, related to the cranberry, is also found on Kaua'i, Maui, and O'ahu, but is less common there than on the island of Hawai'i.

Ancient Hawaiians relished the tart flavor of this native fruit, but, because it belonged to Pele, it was unthinkable to eat any of the berries without first making an offering of them to Pele. If the person was at Halema'uma'u at Kilauea, a branch (or a few berries) would be thrown into the firepit while saying, "Here are your *'ohelo,* Pele. Some I offer to you, some I also eat." Once this was done it was permissible to dine on the refreshing fruit.

'Ohi'a Lehua

'Ohi'a lehua (Merosideros macropus) is a beautiful tree that quickly sprouts and grows on fresh lava flows on the island of Hawai'i. Its scarlet pompom-like flowers are sacred to Pele. (It also flowers in salmon, yellow, pink, and white.) This plant, which can grow in stunted shrubs no more than a few inches high to trees 100 or more feet in height, is a conspicuous presence within Pele's realm.

The *lehua* (the flower of the *'ohi'a*) is also sacred to Hina, Laka and Hi'iaka-i-ka-poli-o-Pele (Pele's younger sister, born of an egg). *Lei* made of these flowers were favored by these goddesses.

When visiting Halema'uma'u (Pele's home at Kilauea on the island of Hawai'i), it was unwise to pluck *lehua* on the way up to the crater. Doing this was believed to bring rain. At the crater, it was picked and offered to Pele, after which it could be made into *lei* and worn.

The hard wood of the *'ohi'a* was used to make furniture, spears, mallets, and floors for structures. It also formed fences around *heiau* (temples), and was used to construct houses and oracle towers within the temple precincts.

Perhaps its most important use was as the material from which images of the *akua* were carved. As a *kino lau* of Ku and Kane, it was the preferred material for creating their images. When the fresh wood is cut, it shows a remarkable resemble to raw meat, which might have led to its sacred character.

The relationship of this tree to both goddesses (Pele, Laka, Hi'iaka, and Hina) and gods (Ku and Kane) may seem puzzling until we recall that worship of some deities was localized. Perhaps it's significant that the wood was used to carve images of Ku and Kane, while the flowers (and the whole tree) were sacred to the female *akua*.

In old Hawai'i, the tree was a symbol of strength due to its ability to survive in harsh climates.

'Olena (Turmeric)

Related to ginger, *'olena (Curcurma domestica)* was probably brought to Hawai'i during the migration period. The underground stems were used to produce a yellow or orange dye and to scent personal articles. The yellow bark cloth that covered the image of Laka on *hula* altars was dyed with *'olena*.

Its most important use was during rites of purification, healing, and exorcism. *'Olena* was mixed with salt water and sprinkled around the area with a prayer to drive away evil, evil spirits, and all defilement. Contact with dead bodies was considered to be extremely defiling. People who had been so soiled were purified with water in which *'olena* and *limu kala* had been mixed.

'Olena was *kapu* to some fishing gods. Thus, their worshippers didn't allow it near their families, canoe sheds, fish hooks or lines, and forbade it as a dye for clothing.

Medicinally, *'olena* was used to treat earache.

Pala'a; Palapala'a

This common fern (*Sphenomeris chinensis;* "lace fern") is a *kino lau* of Hi'iaka. Her sister Pele once sent Hi'iaka on a dangerous mission to retrieve her lover from Kaua'i. While crossing the Puna district of the island of Hawai'i, she was attacked by *mo'o*. Only the skirt that she wore for this express purpose, made of *pala'a*, saved her—the *mo'o* became tangled in the hanging ferns and Hi'iaka defeated them.

Women wore *lei* of *pala'a* to treat all female medical disorders. At ceremonies before dedicating a new war temple, a special priest sprinkled those who would attend the *heiau* with fronds of *pala'a* fern that had been dipped into water. It was a positive omen if the priests were caught in the rain while gathering this fern.

The stems of the *pala'a* fern were also used to make a brownish-red dye.

Pohuehue

Pohuehue is a morning glory *(Ipomoea pes-caprae)* that rambles gracefully across the sand near beaches throughout Hawai'i. This simple plant, which tenaciously grows where few others survive, was much used in old Hawai'i.

The goddess Haumea wore a skirt of *pohuehue* vines around her waist as she fished. It has many other oceanic connections, including one involving surfing. If the waves weren't large enough for good sport, the surfers would whip the sea with these vines while saying (Neal, quoting Fornander):

> *Arise, arise, you great surfs from Kahiki*
> *The powerful curling waves*
> *Arise with the pohuehue*
> *Well up, long raging surf!*

This technique was also occasionally used to kill one who was at sea; i.e., to cause waves large enough to swamp a canoe and drown its occupants. Hawaiians also used the vines to drive fish into nets.

Pohuehue was used in midwifery as well. If a woman was having a very long labor, the *kahuna la'au lapa'au* would pick five budding leaves of the *pohuehue* and pray to Ku to help the woman, then pluck five additional leaves while praying to Hina. These leaves were mashed and rubbed onto the laboring woman's abdomen to cause the child to easily slip out.

Directly after birth (or as needed at any time), the smooth flow of mother's milk was ensured through the use of *pohuehue*. The vines were slapped against the mother's breasts: against the right, Ku was invoked; against the left, Hina. This brought milk.

The plant was sometimes taken internally for medicinal purposes, but in excess it was poisonous.

'Uala (Sweet Potato)

Exactly how the sweet potato, which is also found in South America, reached Hawai'i is uncertain. Many theories have been advanced, all contradictory.

The *'uala (Ipomoea batatas)* was an important food plant in old Hawai'i. Lono was invoked at every stage of planting, tending, and harvesting. Hina was also connected with the sweet potato. On the moon she found a special variety called *hua lani*.

This plant, related to the *pohuehue,* was also used to bring a mother's milk. Two lengths of vine were broken off the plant and placed around the new mother's neck. (The milky white sap that exudes from the broken plant resembles milk.) Alternately, the *'uala* vines were placed in an *ipu* (gourd) of water collected from a spring. At dawn, facing east, the mother slapped her breasts with the vines, praying individually to Ku and Hina to bring her milk.

Wauke (Paper Mulberry)

The *wauke (Broussonetia papyrifera)* is a small tree or shrub that the voyaging Polynesians brought to Hawai'i. *Wauke* is associated with both Hina and Maikoha, from whose body it was said to have grown, and who became *'aumakua* and *akua* of makers of *kapa* (bark cloth, made by processing the bark of the *wauke).*

Wauke's importance in Hawai'i can be simply put: it was used to make cloth and clothing. Contrary to popular opinion, Hawaiians weren't unclothed. They wore a variety of garments, depending on the weather and the occasion. Men wore *malo,* a simple loincloth that consisted of a long, thin strip of that was passed through the legs, wrapped several times around the waist, and tied. Women wore *pa'u* (skirts). The breasts were usually left uncovered because they weren't considered to be sexually stimulating.

Other forms of clothing included the *kihei,* a shoulder cloak worn during cool weather and also by *kahuna pule,* and the *ahu la'i,* a rain cape made of *ki* leaves and worn when walking through the misty mountains.

The manufacture of *kapa* from *wauke* bark was a time-consuming process, and took up much of a Hawaiian woman's day. Women also planted, tended, and harvested this plant, so their lives were intimately tied to *wauke.*

Many varieties of *kapa* were made, of varying fineness or coarseness. *Kapa* was necessary for clothing as well as bed sheets. It was also used in various ceremonial ways. (For more information concerning ritual uses, see Chapter 12.) Large quantities of *kapa* in a household was an indicator of wealth.

CHAPTER FOURTEEN

Dance

A gourd drum hits the ground and is slapped twice by the silver-haired woman who sits before it. She begins chanting. The ʻolapa (dancer) comes to life. She sets her shoulders and head and rhythmically moves her arms, hands, feet, legs, and hips, enacting the story of Pele's migration to Hawaiʻi while the chanter intones behind her. Soon, space and time distorts. Though her steps don't falter, the dancer is aware that she's no longer in control of her body: something far greater has possessed her and now dictates her movements.

"*Ka waʻa a Kane-kalai-honua,*" the chanter states, but the dancer is incapable of hearing her words. She's in a dreamy world of color and movement and sound; removed; distant. Soon, the last words of the chant awaken her. As she moves into the closing position, the ʻ*olapa* feels a sense of loss; of separation. Her rite of worship has ended.

Hula has been greatly misunderstood. What is today presented solely as entertainment was once performed for religious purposes.

Spiritually, *hula* was a ritual of movement and sound (the accompanying chant) in which the dancers worshipped their deities and ritually marked important occasions.

Hula also served as a means of recording and displaying the history of both the people and the deities of Hawai'i. Additionally, dance was a delightful pastime in which both humans and the deities indulged.

The origins of the *hula* are shrouded. Some state that it was created by the goddess Kapo, who was the first dancer and, therefore, the first teacher. However, there are several other explanations of the origin of the *hula*.

One states that a woman became entranced and rhythmically moved while in this state. After she awoke, her friends asked her to teach them these new movements. This became *hula*.

Another possible origin may have been in the observation of nature: the movement of trees and leaves in the wind, the rippling of water, the explosive fury of volcanic eruptions, the movements of birds. All such mesmerizing motions are still recalled in *hula* today, and may indeed have been the original inspiration for the dances.

Yet a fourth possible origination of *hula* was found in the practice of treading the earth of a newly made (and submerged) *kalo* patch. Such treading, which was performed by men, women, and children and treated as a joyous occasion, was necessary to tamp down the ground so that the water wouldn't sink into it. Handy and Handy (see bibliography) speculate that this treading, with its accompanying arm movements (which ensured that the treaders didn't fall as they moved), could have led to the *hula*.

Whatever its origin, *hula* was an integral part of traditional Hawaiian culture and religious ritual.

Ritual *hula* was more than a performance; more than a carefully choreographed dance set to the words of a chanter. In its essence, ritual *hula* was an evocation in which the *mana* of gods, goddesses, lightning, wind, rain, the sea, trees, animals, and birds were brought forth through the dancer. It was this ability to be a conduit of such forces that determined the dancer's skill. Such dances were never done for pure enjoyment or entertainment purposes; they were religious rites.

Indeed, ritual *hula* was as much a dance as it was an invitation to the deities that presided over its practice to enter their dancers. Great *hula* dancers weren't merely inspired; they invoked their deities to enter them. They became the vehicles for the *akua* who took command of the dancer's body and limbs for the duration of the performance.

Who were these deities? Though dancers worshipped many *akua,* it was to Laka that they usually prayed, made offerings, and dedicated themselves. She was the patroness of the art and her dancers kept her *kapu.*

Kapo (who may have been one of Pele's sisters) was also worshipped by some dancers in her guise as a goddess of the *hula,* but her worship in this context may have been less common than that of Laka. One of Emerson's sources stated that Laka was worshipped before Kapo, but that the two goddesses are really one, and this seems to agree with the concept that Kapo was an aspect of Laka. Lono, who is sometimes identified as Laka's husband, was also invoked during *hula.*

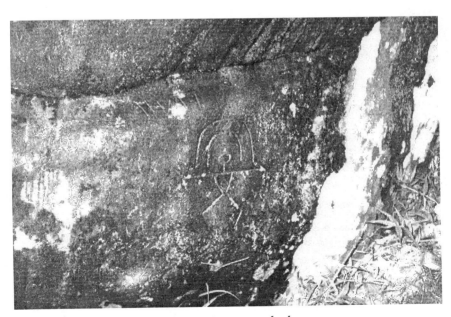

Hawaiian petroglyph

In the *hula* schools, the students learned the prayers to Laka, her *kino lau,* and her *kapu.* Only after these were memorized were dances and chants taught. Keeping Laka's *kapu* was of the utmost necessity, for to break them meant harsh punishment and a lesser chance of perfecting the dance. Among those tabooed things were *ko* (sugar cane), for it roughened the voice (which would inhibit chanting) and would lessen the dancer's skill if consumed.

During training, sex was *kapu,* and personal cleanliness was of the highest importance. Contact with defiling substances (such as corpses) required immediate purification by means of a sea bath and a sprinkling with purificatory water.

Breaking *kapu* ensured the wrath of even the usually gentle Laka (and of the more volatile goddess, Kapo) unless the offender made an offering of *'awa* and a young pig to the goddess.

Upon completion of studies, the dancer was free to perform with a company of dancers for the benefit of the *ali'i,* dance in *heiau,* or move on to learn other occupations.

Both women and men have always danced in Hawai'i. Early reports stated that only men danced in the past, but this seems to have been untrue, and indeed, since *hula* is primarily ruled by goddesses, women may have been its earliest practitioners. Some forms of *hula* were danced only by men, including those performed only in the *heiau* during rituals. Such dances could of necessity only be performed by men, since women were normally forbidden to enter the temples. Many of these dances were concerned with war.

The purposes of ritual *hula* were many. *Hula* was performed at the birth of chiefs, at naming ceremonies, on anniversaries of the birth of the first-born child, and after death to commemorate the deceased. *Hula* for war were apparently quite common as well.

Hula may have also been used to increase human fertility and to ensure an unending supply of food. Additionally, Handy and Handy state that some *hula* might have been performed to bring rain, and *hula* was an important part of the yearly Makahiki celebrations.

One dance, known as *hula pu niu,* was performed by farmers. In the morning a *kumu hula (hula* master) led the farmers in a *hula* accompanied by small coconut drums and other instruments. After the *hula*, the men worked the fields in silence. Another *hula* followed the day's work. There were many other types of *hula*.

Ritual *hula*, then, was usually performed by specially trained dancers under the auspices of Laka and Kapo. It was far more than a pastime; for many, it was a profession. And for all of its practitioners, it was an act of spirituality.

But *hula* wasn't always a solemn rite. Dance was also a common means of self-expression. Persons were known to break into *hula* upon meeting a relative, during 'aha'aina (feasts), and at any time, usually to express joy in a manner that possessed greater eloquence than mere words. Accounts of the deities and of early Hawaiians reveal that both participated in informal *hula* contests, much as they competed in running, wrestling, surfing, sledding, and other sports.

The joy of dancing, whether freely or in set patterns, is one that has been felt by people throughout the world at all times. *Hula* in old Hawai'i was both a pastime and a spiritual ritual.

The change wrought in Hawai'i by exposure to the outside world soon condemned the dance. The *hula* suffered its first blow with the official abolition of the *kapu* system and the destruction of the temples in 1819. *Hula* no longer played a role in religious rites for these rites were no longer openly practiced, but it still enjoyed a measure of popularity as a secular art.

The missionaries, upon arriving in Hawai'i in 1820, saw women and men dancing in abbreviated costumes and "lewdly" moving their hips. Horrified, the missionaries immediately decried *hula* as an indecent dance. This had little effect as first. Soon, however, they found a powerful ally in their quest to destroy this form of expression.

Ka'ahumanu, the favorite wife and widow of Kamehameha I, was baptized a Christian in 1825. She quickly accepted her new teachers' goal of suppressing all expressions of traditional Hawaiian spirituality. Ka'ahumanu passed an edict in 1830 that forbade public *hula*.

Hula became an illegal act. Schools broke up and *kumu hula* (masters of the dance) accepted no new students. In common with many other aspects of traditional Hawaiian culture, *hula* was in danger of being lost.

Fortunately, it wasn't forgotten. *Hula* continued to be taught and practiced in secret within tightly-knit families who recognized *hula* as a way of life, and who could not imagine life without it.

Finally, King David Kalakaua ascended to the throne on February 12, 1874. Dismayed at the rapid disappearance of many aspects of traditional Hawaiian culture, he defied the Christians and declared *hula* to be both a legitimate practice and a vital symbol of Hawaiian culture.

Hula was once again publicly performed. Though it had undergone many changes during its 40-plus years of hidden practice, it quickly regained its former popularity. Its use in ritual, though officially defunct, continued in secret even while *hula* were performed for visiting sailors and at elegant Victorian parties. Female performers soon outnumbered men.

Today, *hula* remains a highly visible symbol of Hawaiian culture. Much has changed, and *hula* is generally performed for non-spiritual reasons. But the very fact that *hula* is still danced in Hawai'i is a tribute to the Hawaiian spirit, and to *hula* is a beautifully powerful means of expressing that spirit.

CHAPTER FIFTEEN

The Menehune

Menehune are the Hawaiian equivalent of brownies, trolls, gnomes, and other diminutive European spirits. They're described as being squat, rather ugly creatures of about two feet in height, with large ears, short noses, long hair, and muscular, strong bodies. They lacked the ability to make fire; loved to eat shrimp, *poi*, cooked *kalo* leaves, and sweet potatoes.

Menehune lived in caves or the forests and had little contact with humans. They delighted in playing many sports and games, including spinning tops made from *kukui* nuts, foot and sled races, arrow shooting, and hand wrestling. At times their amusement at playing such sports was said to cause fish to jump from the sea in alarm, and even to scare birds on neighboring islands.

The *menehune* are said to have migrated to Hawai'i long before the Polynesians. They were expert stone crafters, and are given credit for building many of the ancient temples and fish ponds on all the islands. Near Honolulu alone they built at least nine *heiau* and two fish ponds. They worked only between sunset and sunrise, and finished each project by morning. If it couldn't be completed before dawn, it was left unfinished.

Suspension bridge on Kaua'i near menehune *fish pond*

Precisely why they built such sites is clear: they were hired by chiefs who employed this unusual labor pool. Each *menehune* was usually paid one shrimp for each night's work. Chiefs who had trouble making their people work on construction sites often hired the *menehune* to perform the tasks.

Though invisible to most humans, they could appear to their half-human descendants, for in earlier times *menehune* and humans often mated. The situation became so commonplace that the *menehune* feared the survival of their own kind. These marriages between *menehune* men and Hawaiian women diluted pure *menehune* blood, and so a *menehune* chief on Kaua'i began turning offending *menehune* into stone.

At some point, the king of the *menehune* living on Kaua'i (their number is said to be some 500,000) ordered his people to leave the island and voyage to an unspecified location. Those who had married Hawaiian women were forced to leave behind their wives and children (except their first-born sons). Only one *menehune*, Mohikia, asked to be left on Kaua'i.

Menehune lived on all the islands. On Oʻahu they preferred the lush Manoa and Nuʻuanu valleys as well as Punchbowl. They seem to have been most heavily concentrated on Kauaʻi. Kaumualiʻi, who was the last independent king of Kauaʻi, ordered a census of his island in the early 1800s. In one village his census-takers counted 65 *menehune* residents. Whether these were part *menehune* (descendants of unions between Hawaiian women and *menehune* men) or full *menehune* wasnʻt recorded.

Though tales of the *menehune* are heard everywhere in Hawaiʻi, theyʻre best remembered on Kauaʻi. Examples of their unusual stonework, such as the famous fish ponds near Lihue and the Menehune Ditch (Kika-a-Ola) at Waimea, are still extant. The Kika-o-Ola is an artificially created water course that diverts part of the Waimea stream for agricultural purposes and is faced with shaped, carefully placed stone blocks. This type of stone work is unknown elsewhere in Hawaiʻi except at Puʻuhonua O Honaunau (Place of Refuge at Honaunau, island of Hawaiʻi).

The *menehune* havenʻt been forgotten. Images of them are sold to tourists, childrenʻs books concerning their exploits are published, and even signs designating construction areas in the Honolulu International Airport show a short, nearly naked, big-eared creature wearing a hard hat, tool belt and *lei;* beneath this image are the words: "*Menehune* At Work."

Children have long been warned not to go out at night lest they be frightened by the *menehune.* Some young Hawaiian children ask, in the same breath, if Santa Claus and the *menehune* are real. The *menehune* are an established part of contemporary Hawaiian culture.

Menehune are still thought to supervise construction sites. As recently as 1951, workers moving rocks in Diamond Head Crater arrived each morning to find that their work had been sabotaged during the previous night. The *menehune* had done this, the workers stated, to display their displeasure. A *kahuna* was called in to bless the project.

What lies behind the stories of the *menehune?* Two theories are currently in favor. One states that the *menehune* were the original

Hawaiians: those that migrated to the islands long before the great Polynesian voyages from Tahiti in the twelfth century. This would explain much: the antiquity of their stone work, its form, their inter-marriages with Hawaiian women (who were later migrants), their lack of more sophisticated technology (represented by their legendary inability to make fire), and their continued survival in the islands, especially on Kaua'i. They may have been of slightly shorter stature; hence, the exaggerated stories of their shortness.

Another widely-held theory is that the *menehune* are simply the *maka'aina* (common people) of the Hawaiians themselves. Support for this theory is sound: it was this class in ancient Hawai'i that built *heiau*, fishponds, roads, and other construction projects now credited to the *menehune*. The less privileged, harder working common folk were sometimes shorter than the *ali'i* due to a poorer diet, and this smaller stature could have been exaggerated. *Maka'aina* were also sym-bolically considered to be shorter since they possessed less *mana* than did the *ali'i*.

Heiau, *Big Island, Hawai'i*

Experts state that *heiau* known to have been built by historic chiefs were, after such knowledge had died out among Hawaiians, credited to the *menehune*. This again points to these beings' origination as the *maka'aina*.

The fact that no early Hawaiian-born historians (such as David Malo, Samuel Kamakau, John Papa I'i, and Kepelino) wrote of *menehune* seems to support Luomala's view that they had been nearly forgotten by the time of Western contact, and only in the past 100 years have they been rediscovered and their stories richly embroidered.

Hawaiians were expert storytellers. Perhaps, in time, stories of early migrants (who all but disappeared after the later voyagers arrived in Hawai'i) or tales of the common people were overlaid with so much symbolism and grandeur that even those that had created such tales forgot their origins.

In any case, *menehune* are still sighted in Hawai'i, usually by children who read of their exploits in story books. Some adults insist that the *menehune* can be seen only by psychically sensitive persons, for they're no longer physically present: they exist solely in spirit forms.

Perhaps the popularity of the *menehune* is a veiled acknowledgement of ancient Hawaiian culture, in which such beings were an accepted part of natural science. Today, these magical creatures are certainly a refreshing window into the legendary past of these blessed islands.

CHAPTER SIXTEEN

Ghosts and the Night Marchers

 Ghosts, the spirits of the dead, are known in virtually every culture throughout history. The Hawaiian conception of ghosts was uniquely Polynesian. To understand it it is necessary to examine their conceptions of the human spirit.

The Human Spirit, Soul, and Animating Force

In old Hawai'i, the spirit that resided within humans was called *'uhane*. So, too, was the animating force (that caused the body to move about while alive) and the human soul. All three of these difficult concepts (spirit, animating force, soul) were grouped under the term *'uhane*.

The *'uhane* wasn't permanently attached to the body. It could leave it during sleep via the "spirit hole" *(lua 'uhane)*, near the inner corner of the eye, and return to the body before or upon waking. It was in this spirit form that humans, gods, and goddesses were able to travel long distances in short periods of times. It was considered normal for the 'uhane to travel at night. The adventures of the 'uhane during sleep formed the basis of dreams and nightmares. While travelling, the 'uhane could also converse with the sleeper's 'aumakua to gain their advice. Dreams were studied to reveal omens of the future or warnings from the 'aumakua. When the 'uhane returned to the body through the lua 'uhane, the sleeper often awoke.

Even when the body died and the 'uhane left it, death wasn't necessarily permanent. The soul could be seen fluttering around the body like a butterfly. An expert (kahuna) could catch the 'uhane in a gourd and, through prayer, massage, application of fragrant plants, and a bath, coerce the spirit to reenter its former body. It was reintroduced through the toes and gradually worked back into the entire body, restoring life. (Though the theory and technique is different, this is somewhat similar to using electric shock to restart a heart that has stopped beating. Resuscitation of the dead isn't impossible.)

Sometimes the 'uhane was met by an 'aumakua as it prepared to go to the next world. When this occurred, the 'uhane was returned to its body and the person was restored to life. This occurred when the death was accidental; the person's time had not yet come.

Usually, however, the 'uhane became permanently disconnected at death. But though the body died, the spirit lived on. It left its earthy life forever by travelling the foot paths of the island until it reached a specific spot that usually overlooked the sea. From here it leapt to Po (the underworld).

Each Hawaiian island had its own leaping place (leina) from which the 'uhane of the dead jumped to the underworld. If the leap was successful, the 'uhane entered Po—eternity, the realm of spirits and the 'aumakua (family ancestral deities). If the person had lived a good and honest life, his or her 'aumakua would welcome the 'uhane into their realm.

Po was the Hawaiian underworld; a "sea of eternity," the place of 'aumakua and all the dead. It was often symbolically described as being toward the west, or past the sunset. It was a dark sea, a land of darkness, the world of spirits, a vast, fathomless sea of time.

Po wasn't envisioned as hell. It was more akin to heaven. It possessed streams, forests, and trees (though some say that it was also an ocean). 'Uhane experienced life there much as they had on earth: they ate; learned new games, *hula,* and sports; conversed with their 'aumakua, and generally enjoyed themselves.

This realm was ruled by Milu, a shadowy *akua* about which little is known today. (Christian missionaries, who arrived in 1820 when traditional Hawaiian religion was rapidly dissolving, immediately transformed Po into Hell and Milu into Satan in a zealous effort to stamp out all remaining traces of traditional Hawaiian religion. This resulted in early, post-contact Hawaiian writers such as David Malo misrepresenting their own culture. Much information has been lost.)

Milu may have one time been a chief who, because of his disobedience to the *akua,* was sent by them to rule the underworld. Such stories may show Christian influence.

Lapu (or *'Uhane*): Ghosts

This is, ideally, what happened after death. However, some 'uhane never reached the *leina* (leaping place). Those that had ignored or disobeyed their 'aumakua, who were unloved by their family in life, or who had been wretched individuals whose deaths went unmourned, often never found the *leina* where they could make the jump to Po. Their 'aumakua refused to show the way or to assist the 'uhane of their deceased relatives.

These 'uhane instead wearily wandered about their island home in spirit form. These *lapu* (ghosts; the term 'uhane, in this usage, also means ghost) were known to haunt specific places. They were miserable, homeless spirits that enjoyed neither earthly life or existence in Po. They often dwelled in places that they had known and frequented in life. They ate only spiders and night moths as food (or human food when they could steal it).

A ghost had the same shape as the body that it once possessed, with one exception: the feet of ghosts were often not seen. In fact, few humans could see ghosts, but they were widely feared. Ghosts were believed to have the power to grow larger or smaller, but not to assume animal or other forms.

Though they were feared, ghosts don't seem to have been able to harm humans. Still, many measures were taken to protect life, home, and possessions against ghosts. Food was particularly vulnerable to ghosts; leaves of a variety of banana or *ki* were tied to food packages transported to feasts at night to guard against ghosts. In fact, many Hawaiians avoided eating at night to escape being leapt upon by hungry ghosts.

Ghosts also tripped living persons in the dark, scared animals, voiced warnings of death, knocked on the walls of houses, and threw rocks. Ghosts that haunted wild places often taunted travellers and led them on the wrong paths. Such haunted areas, which were well known on each island, were avoided if at all possible.

Lanahuli above the Pali lookout, associated with Namaka the birdman

There were many signs that ghosts were about. At night, they made their presence known by emitting the odors of the scented *kapa* that had been used to wrap their bones after death.

A pig grunting was a sign of a ghost. Dogs that howled at night for no apparent reason were reacting to the presence of a ghost. A chilly breeze was a common omen that a ghost was present, and might also have been the form that the ghost had taken. Other forms that ghosts might assume include clouds, birds, and rocks.

Even fish weren't safe from ghosts. Certain fish (*uoa*, a type of mullet, and *weke*, a surmullet) sometimes have an unpleasant taste. This is created by ghosts that inhabit these fishes' heads. In eating one of these fish, the diner was instructed to throw a bone from the dinner into the ocean, saying "Here is your share, O Pahulu." (Pahulu was a "chief" of ghosts.)

The phosphorescent glow *(weli)* occasionally seen on the waves of the ocean is also caused (indirectly) by ghosts. A man, Punia, captured several ghosts in a net in the ocean and "killed" them. Their "deaths" caused the sea to glow at night, and also imparted a strong odor to the fish *kala* and *palani*.

Ghost-Testing

Sometimes, ghosts would be so like living people that tests were necessary to determine their true nature. One was quite simple. A gourd or wooden bowl was filled with water and the suspected ghost asked to look into it. A ghost would cast her or his reflection on the surface of the water; a living human would not.

Or, large leaves of the 'ape vine were placed on the ground, and the suspected ghost asked to walk over them. The living person's feet would shred the leaves; the ghost wouldn't. A third method was quite simple: the suspected person was startled. It would instantly vanish if it was a ghost.

Ka Huaka'i O Ka Po: The Night Marchers

Even after death and entrance to Po, the 'uhane possessed the ability to return to places that it had known in life. Such 'uhane, when they temporarily returned, appeared exactly as they had while alive.

On certain nights each month, especially Akua, Ku, Kane, and Lono, ghostly processions sometimes take place. (See Appendix: The Hawaiian Lunar Calendar.) These are groups of "night marchers;" spirits of long-dead Hawaiians that return on such nights. Such processions might included the 'uhane of dead chiefs, warriors, priests and priestesses, 'aumakua, and akua.

They walk the islands at night, striking terror into the hearts of those that they meet, for all who are discovered witnessing this spectral spectacle are immediately struck dead, unless caring 'aumakua were among them to grant protection to their living family members. Death is dealt to living witnesses by the guard that usually marched at the front or rear of the procession.

Ka huaka'i o ka Po are usually led by men bearing torches that blaze with an unearthly glow. The sound of chanting, a drum beat, or the eerie music of a nose flute may have been heard. Alternately, they may pass in total silence.

Those out at night who hear the tell-tale drums or see the glow of the torches through the trees have two options to save themselves from death: tear off all clothing and lie face down in the dirt (this amuses the marchers, who pass on without inflicting death), or, at the very least, hide until the procession passed by. Eventually, it might disappear, or its members might engage in sports on a nearby flat piece of land. But by the first light of dawn they vanish.

Marches of akua and 'aumakua were brilliantly lit; those of chiefs less so. There were apparently many types of processions. Precisely why the 'uhane marched is unclear. Perhaps the 'uhane were simply homesick and wished to visit the homes that they enjoyed during earthly existence.

Sightings of the night marchers continue in Hawai'i today, and accounts are occasionally published in newspapers of persons who are frightened by "*malo*-clad warriors."

I've been unable to discover whether the Night Marchers are a relatively modern phenomenon (i.e., first seen in the last 170 years) or of ancient origin. In either case, they're known throughout Hawai'i.

Lapu in Hawai'i Today

Ghosts are still present in Hawai'i. This isn't difficult to understand since hundreds of thousands of Hawaiians are buried there as are hundreds of thousands of non-Hawaiians. Hawaiians didn't accept that spirit died following the death of the body; hence, the spirits are still present.

One area in Kaneohe on Oahu was known to have been frequented by ghosts. A small shopping center that was built there was haunted. Many locals wouldn't go near the place after dark.

It is on Kaua'i that stories of ghosts most frequently circulate. Kaua'i, the oldest of the Hawaiian islands, is also the most steeped in ancient lore. Many stories of hauntings originate in the new hotels and resorts that have been built in Kaua'i in recent years, and it's theorized that the spirits are unpleased at the disturbance of sacred sites.

One condominium complex was built on the grounds of an old Hawaiian temple. Guests staying in the rooms complained of doors opening and banging shut and other strange phenomena. *Kahuna* were called in seven times to bless the property. The seventh apparently did the trick; no more ghostly trouble occurred.

PART THREE

Magic and Sorcery

Hawaiian sunrise

Hana Aloha

"Love work," as this term is translated into English, was concerned with creating love within another person, strengthening an existing relationship, and breaking love spells. It was often performed by special priests, *kahuna aloha* ("love experts"). But the lovestruck person may have also prayed to her or his *'aumakua,* to the *akua,* or sought the help of a family member knowledgeable about the ways that bring love.

Most love rites were designed to make the victim so infatuated with the person for whom the rite was performed that she or he couldn't eat or sleep until the two of them were united.

Many *akua* were invoked for love, among them Laka and Makanikeoe, a wind god who was specially associated with bringing love. When invoked, he would disturb the victim's nights. Makanikeoe was also an *akua* of certain plants and could take the body of a tree. A piece of this tree was used in love charms. However, any who took a branch from this tree would experience strange voices and visions.

Plants were often used in *hana aloha. Pili* grass, whose name means "to cling; to adhere," was used for this symbolism. So too was one variety of banana, the *lele* ("fly away"). It was used in love magic to make the lovestruck one's emotions fly to the intended victim. Another plant used in *hana aloha* was the *milo (Thespesia populnea),* a native tree. The seeds, flowers, and leaves were used.

Sugarcane *(ko)* is perhaps the most famous of the love-inducing plants. In old Hawai'i, many dozens of varieties of *ko* were cultivated. Each was distinctive in form, growing habits, and coloration. Four of these types, *manu lele* ("flying bird"), *papa'a* ("hold fast"), *pili mai* ("come here"), and *lahi* ("thin; frail; delicate") were widely used in *hana aloha.* Unfortunately, most old cane varieties have today been lost.

Manu lele sugar cane was used to make love "fly" to the targeted person. A *kahuna aloha* prayed over the sugar cane, dedicating it to Makanikeoe. The one who had consulted the *kahuna* then ate the cane and blew in the direction of the beloved. The wind god carried the love *mana* to the desired person. Once touched by it, she or he was suffused with love. This was usually performed together with a cane of the *pili mai* variety.

The *papa'a* variety was similarly used. One source, however, says that it had a special application: women who were suspicious of their mate's fidelity would take this cane to a *kahuna,* who prayed that the relationship would be steady, and that the man would *papa'a* (hold fast) to her. The prepared cane was then fed to the suspected wandering man.

Pili mai was used as the *manu lele,* while the *lahi* variety of sugar was used for quick dalliances rather than for lasting relationships.

A fifth type of sugar cane, *lau kona* or *lau kona kona* (leaf of the Kona wind; a gusty, hot, winter wind) was used to break the power of *hana aloha.* The person who thought that he or she was a victim of the practice brought this cane to a *kahuna,* who prayed over it to *kala hana aloha* ("loosen the love work"). The victim then ate the cane so that the infatuation would be blasted away like a leaf in the furious Kona wind.

In an similar area, women would use the fragrant flower clusters of the male *hala* plant as a love charm or as an aphrodisiac, to stimulate the man of her choosing.

Other objects beside plants were used in love work. At least two types of fish were found to contain the correct *mana.* The *ahole,* a common shore fish, was one of these. Its use in *hana aloha* is preserved in the statement *he ahole ka i'a, hole ke aloha* ("*ahole* is the fish, love is restless").

Another fish used in love magic was the *ulua.* Since this fish was a suitable substitute for a man in rites of human sacrifice, it was also suitable to draw a man to a woman. Yet a third sea creature, the sea cucumber or sea slug *(loli),* was used as an offering to secure love.

One extraordinary example of *hana aloha* originated on the island of Maui. A *kahuna aloha* prayed that the victim would fall in love with the lovestruck client. The client then stood with his or her back to the wind holding a flower, in a place where the victim was soon likely to pass. Spitting upon the flower, the client said, "Spit! You come seeking me of your own accord!" and let the flower drop to the ground. When the victim walked near the flower, she or he would be so possessed with love that he or she would search for the one who had the spell performed.

Fragments of the types of prayers used in *hana aloha* have survived:

E hiaala, e hele iaiia e ululku ai,
e moe 'ole ai kona po.

(Keep awake, go to him and disturb, so
his night is sleepless.)

The following was said over a piece of *manu lele* sugar cane:

Makani-ke-oe
Hono a lele
Lele ke aloha
Pili ia (inoa)
'ilaila 'e pili ai
'A moe 'ole kona pa

(Makani-ke-oe (The wind/love god)
(The) joining flies
The love flies
This pertains to (name)
There it will be in contact
And sleepless are his/her nights.)

'Ana'ana *(Sorcery)*

This is the most famous of ancient Hawaiian magical practices: the art of sending sickness, insanity, or death. Such rituals were conducted by the *kahuna 'ana'ana* (expert sorcerer). The *kahuna 'ana'ana* wasn't an outcast of society, for he was in service to the *ali'i* and was supposed to use his art only for the good of the *ali'i*. In a western sense, he was the royal executioner. (Most of them seem to have been men; thus, my use of "he" and "him" above.)

The rite of sending death to another was usually conducted with the use of *maunu* ("bait"); that is, something that had been in intimate contact with the victim, such as hair, nail clippings, saliva, or a garment that the victim had worn. These objects contained some of the victim's *mana* and so could be used to affect the person. (This is precisely why such personal objects were usually safeguarded to keep them out of the hands of sorcerers.)

The rite itself was accomplished with prayers to any or all of the sorcery *akua,* including Kapo, Uli, Ka-alae-a-Hina, and others, and by the recitation of death-producing prayers.

Some who practiced this art naturally enjoyed it and needlessly killed. Such *kahuna,* however, were punished by the *akua* and their *'aumakua* with a frightful death, such as decapitation, or the most ignoble of all: dying on the path with the grease of his body flowing onto the ground. Though it may seem absurd, the actions of the *kahuna 'ana'ana* were indeed governed by a strict moral code. In a sense he was a spiritual warrior who killed his chief's enemies with spells, not with spears, axes, or clubs.

The death-dealing *kahuna,* who are still feared today by some in Hawai'i, held an important role in ancient Hawaiian society. It was a noble profession. Though they were feared, they were a necessary evil. Killing for the chief was positive; killing for joy or lust was negative. Additionally, the *kahuna 'ana'ana* was also instructed in the arts of curing and healing, and may have at times resorted to poisoning his chief's enemies.

Such priests were always subject to countersorcery, in which their curses were returned to them by their victims or by other sorcerers.

However important these experts were, they were far from the only type of *kahuna.*

Ho'ounauna *(Sending Spirits)*

This practice was performed for both positive and negative purposes. Sending the spirit of a deceased relative to give warning or to perform other acts of mercy was a form of *ho'ounauna.* So, too, was the act of sending *akualele* (flying gods or spirits) to bring destruction on one's enemies.

The *akualele* resembled fireballs flying through the air. Such sorcery was only practiced at night. Long ago, the island of Moloka'i was

City of Refuge, Hawai'i

known as the home of sorcerers. The *kahuna* of Moloka'i sent *akualele* by scraping images made of magically poisonous wood to their enemies.

Fortunately, the spirit could be returned to vent its destruction upon its *kahu* ("keeper;" the sorcerer who had sent it). A guiltless person was able to return any destructive spirit simply by saying the words *ho'i no 'ai ikou kahu* ("go back and destroy your keeper").

Kuni *(To Burn; a Rite of Revenge)*

This is a ritual in which the family of a victim of *'ana'ana* could take revenge on the death-dealing sorcerer. It was performed by the *kahuna kuni,* who was also usually a *kahuna* as well.

If necessary, divination was performed to discover the identity of the offending *kahuna 'ana'ana.* Once this was determined, the rite began.

Offerings were made. Some part of the victim was burned with prayer. The ashes were then sprinkled on a place where the sorcerer was likely to walk, or in the area where he bathed. The incantations and *mana* ensured that the sorcerer would die for his misdeeds.

Protection and Exorcism

Surrounded as they were by practitioners of sorcery, by persons of ill will, ghosts and spirits, and the sorcery *akua,* it was only natural for Hawaiians to ritually protect themselves.

The most available and widely-used method was known as *pi kai,* the sprinkling of specially prepared water to disperse evil. Disturbances in the home could be relieved by *pi kai,* ghosts were sent away by the sprinkling of the sacred water, and healings (of diseases created by evil spirits) speeded.

Plants were also used for their protective *mana. Ki* leaves were worn for protection when travelling in dangerous areas, and also guarded food from ghosts. The leaves of *'ape (Alocasia macrorrhiza)* were prized for their protective qualities, due to the irritating sap of the leaves. It was placed under sleeping mats at night to protect against ghosts, and was placed under the mats on which sick persons rested for the same purpose. Curiously, it was never planted near houses out of the belief that it would bring sickness to their inhabitants. A third plant, a indigenous species of Pandanus *(hala pia),* was used to exorcise evil spirits. (More protective plant lore can be found in Chapter 13.)

Many fish also possessed the correct *mana* for protection. The *ahole* was commonly used to ward off evil spirits, for its name means "to strip away" (i.e., to remove evil). It was usually offered for this purpose.

The *ahole* fish were also placed under the posts of new houses to guard them from evil influences. This was considered to be so effective that, if a *kahuna* entered a home that had been so protected and predicted trouble for its residents, the *kahuna* would die for his lies. A type of shrimp *(mahiki)* was also widely used, with prayer *(pule mahiki),* to drive away evil spirits.

Everyday prayers to the 'aumakua and akua also usually included pleas for protection and long life, and so prayer was also protective in nature. Indeed, many times family 'aumakua would appear to warn of impending danger.

Other Types of Magic

To Induce Pregnancy

Two *hinalea* fish were wrapped in *ki* leaves and cooked on the coals of a fire. The first fish was dedicated to Ku and the second to Hina. Before the woman desiring to reproduce ate the first fish, the *kahuna* prayed to Ku, asking that he grant the woman a child. If a boy was desired, the *kahuna* included in his prayer a man's duties, such as fishing, farming, or house-building. If a girl was wanted, such activities as *kapa*-making, plaiting, and other activities were mentioned. The same prayer is made over the second fish, though it was then directed to Hina. Both fish were then eaten by the woman, after they'd been empowered by the words of the *kahuna*.

For Excellence in Hula

The graduate would offer a *kumu* (goatfish) so that complete mastery *(kumu)* of the dance would be attained.

For General Success in All Undertakings

The fish *napili,* which was a common food fish, was also used in magic to attract success. The *napili* fish clings to rocks; hence, its *mana* lent this power to new homes, to which success and happiness would cling, to new-born babies, to whom blessings would adhere, and to anyone who was beginning a new venture. Such fish were specially prepared with prayer and eaten or given as offerings to the *akua* or *'aumakua.* (This fish was known as *nopili* on Kaua'i.)

To Attract Fish

The *hinakea,* a grayish-white stone with one flat side and one rounded side, was placed on coral to attract fish that bore a resemblance to the stone's color.

For Safe, Restful Sleep

Thin, flat, water-smoothed black stones were placed beneath *lauhala* pillows to halt the wanderings of the *'uhane* (the human spirit and soul) during sleep.

CHAPTER EIGHTEEN

Prophecy and Dreams

Unfettered by the rigid, materially-based conventions of Western culture, Hawaiians accepted the existence of psychic awareness, of dreams that predicted the future, and of visions sent by the dead.

These concepts were probably brought to Hawai'i from its settlers' original island homes. Some are based upon simple observation: a sleeper has a dream, sees that it contains a message, and discovers that this message is true.

Such discoveries of new sources of information would have been highly prized. The fact that this information wasn't gathered through the "ordinary" five senses wasn't of concern, since Hawaiians didn't limit human perception to that received by the skin, eyes, ears, nose, and tongue. Indeed, they seem to have had a deep spiritual connection with nature and their universe, and such links are often intuitively and emotionally sensed, not physically felt, heard, or seen.

This chapter discusses some of the ways in which these methods of information gathering were in use among ancient Hawaiians.

Ike Papalua ("Twice Seeing;" Psychic Awareness)

What we term "psychic awareness" was known among old Hawaiians. It was considered to be a rare gift and those proficient in the talent were the recipients of special *mana* from the *akua*. The ability to know future events or what was simultaneously occurring at some distance from the knower couldn't be learned, it was inborn. Such persons didn't observe omens in the clouds, watch the stars, or use predictive tools. They didn't perform divination to discover future events. They simply knew. (This term also refers to supernatural knowledge and the ability to communicate with spirits.)

Today, we'd call such persons psychics. In Hawai'i, they often became *kaula* (prophets).

Kaula

As with most special talents, an aptitude for prophecy was usually discovered at an early age. Perhaps some *ho'ailona* (omen) pointed to the birth of a *kaula*. Or perhaps a family member realized the child's gifts. Some *kaula* received training in various skills and became *kahuna*, but many did not. Others became dedicated to specific deities (on the Island of Hawai'i, particularly to Pele). Some lived as hermits in wild and lonely places, but most chose to remain with their family and friends.

Not much is known about the role of the prophet in society, though some became famous for specific, precise predictions. Female *kaula* were also recognized, but again little information concerning them is available. However, it seems that female *kaula (kaula na wahine)* were also recognized in youth. When mature, they were even allowed to enter the *heiau* (usually *kapu* to women) and participate in rituals with the men. Only female *kaula* who were also *kahuna pule* could enter the precincts of the *kapu* temples. When in ritual there, they often wore a white *malo* (loincloth), a garment of sacredness usually reserved for the male *kahuna* priests. Such women lived the equivalent of men's lives.

Predictions made by some *kaula* became quite famous, particularly when they were concerned with chiefs and proved to be true. Fornander (see Bibliography) states that a female *kaula* named Wa'ahia was so famous in her day that merely mentioning her name was sufficient to recall her entire story. Unfortunately, this story was never recorded and has now been lost.

Moe 'Uhane (Dreams)

In contrast to psychic awareness, everyone had access to information through dreams. Dreams were recognized as significant because during sleep, the *'uhane* (the personal, immortal spirit and soul) wandered free from the body, visiting relatives, meeting with other spirits, and having numerous adventures. It was also while dreaming that communication between the sleeper and the *'aumakua* was the most clear and direct.

Entering Waimea Canyon

Significant dreams could be both requested and spontaneous. If a person was experiencing a problem, she or he might pray to the 'aumakua directly before sleep to reveal an answer in a dream. Upon waking the next morning, the dream was analyzed, layer upon layer, to reveal the 'aumakua's response.

Similarly, specialists requested dreams that gave assistance with particular professional problems: a healing *kahuna* might ask for a dream that revealed the diagnosis of a patient as well as the appropriate treatment.

Spontaneous dreams were just that—dreams that simply occurred. Such dreams often carried powerful symbolic value and were carefully studied to reveal possible meanings and to forecast future events.

Remedies for simple sicknesses and physical conditions were often received in dreams, as well as information concerning distant relatives. New chants and *hula* were also received in dreams. Usually, however, dreams were warnings of future sickness or death, or omens of good fortune.

Interpretation of dreams was a commonplace activity. The strength of *ohana* (family) was such that one member's dream might affect the entire family (in fact, one could dream for (not about) another).

Interpretations of dreams widely varied. Among some families, certain symbols were considered fortunate; in other families, unfortunate. However, many dreams had specific meanings known to all.

If a dream foretold an evil or unfortunate future, the dreamer could, upon waking, pray to the 'aumakua to alter the future by severing the dream's influence.

Akaku (Visions)

During waking hours, advice and warning could unexpectedly come even to non-psychic persons. Visions, *akaku,* could be experienced at any time. So, too, could *'ulaleo:* voices or sounds that emanated from other than normal means.

Such visions and voices were usually of a warning nature, such as "Don't go down that path," or "Go home; your baby is sick." Strange lights may have appeared over the water that led fishermen to richer areas of the sea. Voice and vision didn't always come together.

Visions were usually of deceased relatives who had come to counsel or to warn their beloved descendants. The one appearing was usually known and loved by the person to whom it appeared. True visions and voices were always of a helpful nature.

The *akua* and *'aumakua* were also seen in visions. Pele is perhaps the most widely-seen Hawaiian deity of our time. She may appear in the form of a beautiful young woman dressed in white, as an old woman, or as a white dog (one of her *kino lau*).

Visions and voices were accepted as commonplace in old Hawai'i. Though the messages sent might be frightening, there was nothing frightening about seeing one's *'aumakua* or beloved family members who had made the leap to the underworld. Though those who returned were, in a sense, ghosts, they were also family, and so weren't feared.

There seems to have been no connection between such voices and visions and psychic awareness. The latter was a rare gift, while anyone could experience visions or hear the voices of their concerned, deceased family members.

Information obtained in any of these three ways was considered to be just as viable and important as that acquired through any other method.

CHAPTER NINETEEN

Divination, Omens, and Possession

Hawaiians' quest to know the future didn't depend solely on dream interpretation and the utterings of prophets *(kaula)*. People also watched nature and everyday life to attain glimpses of tomorrow. Since all nature (clouds, whirlwinds, the ocean, stars and comets, and the earth itself) consisted of manifested *akua,* it could speak to those who would hear. Observation of omens was an integral part of early Hawaiian culture.

When even these methods failed, or when the seeker could no longer wait, more direct method of divination was used. Divination (the ritual use of specific tools to determine the future) was generally the province of *kahuna* and other experts, to whom the populace would go to receive information.

A third method of attaining guidance was that of *noho,* possession, in which an *'aumakua* was invited to "perch" upon the family medium and speak of the future.

All three of these techniques will be discussed in this chapter.

Ho'ailona (Omens)

Omens were carefully observed in old Hawai'i. Several classes of *kahuna* spent much of their time discerning future events by studying the clouds, the skies and stars, sudden winds, the movements of plants, unusual waves, the behavior of birds and animals, and other natural phenomena.

Some omens were quite explicit: dark clouds indicated rain. Others were far subtler and required expert interpretation. Fortunately, Hawai'i had many skilled observers and interpreters of omens. They predicted everything from the fall of the local ruling chief to drought, rain, death, storms, the outcome of battles, times for fishing, the sex of unborn children, and other occurrences. Such *kahuna* were often favorites of the chiefs.

Among these experts were the *kahuna kilokilo,* who watched the skies and stars; the *kahuna nana uli,* who predicted the weather and predicted from the weather; the *kahuna kilo makani,* observer of the winds; and the *kahuna kilo hoku,* who studied the stars and the moon for information.

Cloud Omens

Hawaiian *kahuna* gleaned much information from the shape, appearance, height from the horizon, color, movement, and groupings of clouds. When reading clouds they also took into consideration the direction, time of day, and the appearance of the sea. The moon, rain, and other celestial phenomena were also observed.

Pointed cumulus clouds foretold rain and storms. White clouds that rose from the sea or that lay close to larger cloud banks were indicators of rain in Kona (Island of Hawai'i). Yellow, heavy clouds hanging low on the horizon indicated fine weather ahead.

Rainbow Omens

Rainbows were often seen as signs of death, but they had many other possible meanings. A rainbow might betray the presence of a disguised *ali'i*. During birth, it foretold an especially blessed baby. At other times, it could warn of an impending separation of some kind.

A rainbow appearing while on a journey (to the fields, to a canoe, to the forests to gather bird feathers) indicated bad luck.

Rainbows were also omens that the *akua* were watching the activities of the chiefs, and some believed that rainbows that were predominantly red indicated that their *'aumakua* were near and watchful. Rainbows predicted the weather as well: seen during rain they indicated a short shower; accompanied by wind, they predicted an extended rain.

Hoku *(Star) Lore and Omens*

Traditional Hawaiian culture derived a great deal of information from the stars and planets, though much of this has been lost.

Astronomical knowledge was important to the Hawaiians for a number of reasons. The stars were among their main navigational tools; in fact, the star we known as Sirius was named Hoku-ho'okele-wa'a ("canoe-guiding star"). Stars also determined the start of ritual periods (the rising of the Pleiades, Na-ka-a-Makali'i, marked the commencement of the Makahiki celebration) and denoted correct times for planting and fishing. The positions of the stars also, in part, determined the calendar.

Kahuna kilo observed the movements of the planets and stars and, according to their relative positions, predicted future events. Conjunctions of certain stars and planets signalled the time for propitious battle. The direction in which meteors flashed across the sky indicated the direction to be watched for the approach of enemy forces. The appearance of comets *(hoku welowelo)* was also a significant omen.

The movements of the planets were particularly watched. Hawaiians were well acquainted with Mercury (Ukali), Venus (Mana-nalo),

Mars (Hoku-'ula), Jupiter (Ka'a-wela or Ho'o-ma-nalo-nalo), and Saturn (Makulu).

One star in particular, Holo pina'au (identified in the *Hawaiian Dictionary* as perhaps being a variant name for Mars), was closely watched in its position to a circle of twelve other stars. Its movements in relation to this group—travelling to the east or the west of the starry circle—revealed many future events. If Holo pina'au entered the circle of stars itself, disaster was foretold for the chiefs.

Other Sky Omens

A small ring around the moon indicated wonderful fishing, while a large ring foretold stormy weather ahead. If rain had fallen for many days but the stars didn't appear to twinkle one night, fine weather would prevail in a few days. (Rain is usually sporadic and moves on; thus, the stars could indeed be seen at night even during rainy periods.)

"Dry" thunder (that which is unaccompanied by rain) was rare, and, if lengthy, was a sign of an impending volcanic eruption to the people of the Ka-'u district of the Island of Hawai'i. A clap of thunder usually accompanied the birth of a new chief, and was an omen of this occurrence.

Whirlwinds were warnings of impending disaster and sudden breezes indicated the presence of ghosts or spirits. Rain, if accompanied by lightning, thunder, and wind, wouldn't be lengthy. A red western sky at sunset indicated that clear weather was ahead. A dangerously high surf foretold the imminent death of a chief.

Everyday Omens

Meteorological and metaphysical advice from expert observers was undoubtedly invaluable to farmers, fishermen, navigators, and all people but other omens could be detected by everyone.

Everyday life offered many opportunities for discovering the future. Some of these omens and their attendant messages are remarkably akin to those known in Europe; many omens, particularly those involving the human body, are known worldwide.

Animal Omens

Unusual behavior in animals and birds provided insights into the future. Roosters, which Hawaiians brought to the islands as a source of food, frequently made predictions. A rooster crowing too early in the morning was an omen of the impending arrival of canoes on the beach nearby. A rooster crowing near the door of a house indicated visitors.

Dogs howling at night for no apparent reason indicated the presence of ghosts, or were signs that a death had occurred. Whales swimming against the wind foretold clear weather ahead. If they swam with the wind, a storm was approaching.

Birds were also closely observed. Those that hovered over humans were seen as signs of warning. Owls and mudhens frequently gave guidance: they warned of danger either ahead on the path or back at home by their sudden appearance and cries. Mudhens croaking near a house after dark presaged trouble.

Incredibly vast numbers of fish, far greater than normal, indicated an impending unusual event. This might be death or simply a shift of power among the ruling chiefs. A swordfish swimming ashore of its own volition was an omen that someone related to (and who worshipped) Ku'ula, the primary fishing god, was about to die.

For anyone swimming in the ocean, a sudden rise in water temperature was a sure sign that a shark was near.

Fishing Omens

Fishermen also observed omens. Their most trusted source of omens was the *uhu,* the parrot fish. Its movements revealed whether the fisherman's spouse was observing fishing *kapu* back at home (vital to obtaining a good catch). If this fish frolicked about in the sea, it indicated a lack of solemnity at home—a serious breach of the *kapu* that had to be followed to ensure a successful fishing expedition.

Two *uhu* rubbing noses indicated that the fisherman's spouse was flirting with another man. Such omens sent most fishermen back home—they'd catch no fish that day.

Black sand beach, Big Island, Hawai'i

Other negative omens included suddenly breaking a fish hook (revealing that the fisherman's woman was having sex with another man) and a fish hook that freed itself from its line.

Omens from the Human Body

Ringing in the ears or a "shivering scalp" indicated that someone was speaking of the afflicted. Throbbing in the feet betokened an upcoming journey. A foot or leg that suddenly went numb for no good reason was a sign of an impending journey or the sudden arrival of a visitor. Stumbling on a journey was an omen of misfortune.

Meeting a lame, blind, or deformed person while on the path was a negative omen, but encountering two such persons was favorable. Meeting anyone carrying bananas while going off to fish meant that no fish would be caught.

A *kahuna la'au lapa'au,* upon journeying to heal a sick person, would return home if she or he met a man on the footpath with his hands crossed behind his back. This indicated a cure was impossible. If a *kahuna* was eating when called to heal someone, it was an omen that he wasn't the correct expert for the case and shouldn't accept it.

Omens are still observed today by some persons in Hawai'i.

Hailona (Divination)

Divination is the practice of using certain tools to gain insights into current situations or glimpses of future events. Hawaiian *kahuna* excelled at divination.

Proficiency in this art was necessary for many experts in various fields. A medical *kahuna* might divine the nature or origin of an illness. A *kahuna aloha* could determine whether love was genuine or simply infatuation. A *kahuna kuni* performed rites to discover the identity of a person who had wrongly prayed another to death. A *kahuna kuhikuhi pu'uone* might use divination in finding a site for a new temple.

Divination was also used to determine the outcome of battles and, based on the results, might lead the warring chiefs to voluntarily halt fighting.

There were many methods used to predict the future. One simple one was to ritually gather *'awa* roots (see Chapter 13), prepare the beverage, pour it into a cup, drink a bit of the liquid, and gaze into the remainder left in the cup.

Such divinations were common among the *kahuna la'au lapa'au*. Before taking a patient, the herbal healer would perform an *'awa* divination. After pouring the drink into a gourd used for divination (*ipu 'olelo*), the *kahuna* would study the *'awa* to determine the outcome of any treatment. Signs included the *'awa* swirling around or remaining motionless.

Or, the stiff midrib of a *ki* leaf would be placed over the gourd or a coconut cup. One side (as divided by the midrib) represented the *kahuna*; the other, the patient. *'Awa* was poured in. Bubbles were favorable signs; lack of bubbles, unfavorable. Many other signs could also appear to assist the healer in deciding whether or not to work with the patient. Such rites were also performed with rain water and the liquid from coconuts.

Alternately, the *'awa* was ritually prepared in the hollowed-out trunk of a *hala* (see Chapter 13) for diagnostic purposes. The patient and his or her family were each given a cup of the liquid. The *kahuna* gazed into each cup, searching for a bubble that rose in the center of the cup. In this bubble the *kahuna* could see an image of the cause of the disease that had afflicted the patient.

A similar divination involved the use of two *'ilima* flowers. They were set afloat in a cup of water. If the flowers clung to each other, signs were favorable. If they floated apart, unfavorable. A *kahuna* who had consulted this oracle and had received a negative sign wouldn't accept a case. (This was also used to determine if love truly existed between two individuals, whether a *kahuna* should treat a patient, and for other reasons.)

Untrained baby pigs were used for divination, especially to determine whether an unknown person who claimed to be an *ali'i* was truly a chief. After prayers, the pig was unleashed. If an *ali'i* was present, it would quickly go to him or her, rest, and fold its legs under its body. Pigs were also used to discover the location of the bones of the *ali'i*.

Divination involving stones has been recorded. A thief about to steal went to a *kahuna* for advice. The priest randomly placed two piles of pebbles beneath a *kapa*. One of these piles represented the thief; the other, his intended victim. The pebbles were then counted by twos, to determine the success or failure of the impending robbery. There were other forms of divination involving pebbles.

Noho (Possession)

Spirit possession was an accepted aspect of traditional Hawaiian culture. Anyone could become possessed by a spirit, an *'aumakua*, or even an *akua*. Such possession could be voluntary or involuntary, helpful or harmful, partial or total. It was always a temporary phenomenon.

Voluntary Possession

Long before the fad of spiritualism swept Europe and America, Hawaiians were contacting the spirits of deceased ancestors for advice, for the 'aumakua were ritually invited to speak to their descendants during a ritual resembling a seance (minus the "apports," "ectoplasm," hymns, and fees charged). Most families had at least one *haka* (medium) through which their 'aumakua could speak and assist in troublesome matters. These occasions were prayerful rituals and had no association with sorcery or magic.

After offering 'awa and chanting prayers to the gods and goddesses, a family member known as a *kahu* (in this sense, the ritualist presiding over the ceremony; the "spirit keeper") prayed and chanted to the 'aumakua, inviting him or her to take possession of the *haka.* The medium might sip 'awa to assist the possession.

When possessed by the 'aumakua, the *haka* spoke in a different voice and in a way that firmly identified the specific 'aumakua who had returned. The *haka* answered questions asked of the 'aumakua by the *kahu.* Unlike modern Western seances, such rituals weren't performed in darkened rooms.

Haka were usually chosen in childhood by omens that pointed to the birth of a new medium. They were carefully trained in the art. Some of them became *kaula* (prophets in service to the *ali'i),* but most worked only for their families, and never lost their ability *(mana)* to perform as mediums unless they broke some *kapu* that offended the 'aumakua.

The *haka* weren't the only ones who voluntarily submitted to possession for the good of others. At least some of the *kaula* were undoubtedly possessed while predicting the future, and it seems clear that the *kahuna* who ascended the oracle tower in the temple and spoke for the deities were possessed.

Involuntary Possession

Possession could take place at any time without warning. A person's *'aumakua* might partially (and unexpectedly) possess a surfer, fisherman, or warrior to lend assistance while surfing, fishing, or fighting. Great bursts of energy and displays of unusual skill were attributed to partial possession by the *'aumakua*. Additionally, the *'aumakua* could unexpectedly possess a person in times of danger or illness to protect or to lend strength to the person.

The *akua* were also known to lend their assistance: Laka, the goddess of the *hula,* often possessed her dancers, and Pele possessed her prophets on regular occasions, usually to warn of impending eruptions.

Not all involuntary possessions were this pleasant. Disease was understood to be the result of an evil spirit inhabiting a person's body, and much of the cure lay in the removal of the offending spirit (that had been sent by another person or *kahuna*). Additionally, persons who had performed outrageous or anti-social acts were usually believed to have been temporarily possessed.

Another form of involuntary possession also existed. Unscrupulous *kahu* could also send spirits of the dead (artificially created ghosts, *'unihipili*) to torment or to possess the living. These persons sometimes attacked others at will. Persons thus possessed were sent to a *kahuna* for removal of the spirit.

Spirit possession, then, could be positive or negative. For the Hawaiians, it was an accepted fact of life.

CHAPTER TWENTY

Birth Omens

Hawaiians were particularly interested in the moon, both as a highly visible calendar and also as an indicator of character traits for those born during each of the lunar months. This information was apparently compared with that obtained from the day of the lunar month upon which the birth occurred, as each day also indicated specific future traits. From the incomplete information that was recorded, we can gain a fairly complete picture of the influence of the month and moon *(mahina)* on human character. (Many of these traits appear to be concerned solely with males.)

Note that our months don't precisely fit with those recognized in Hawai'i, due to internal structural differences. Only approximate comparisons can be made. (For more information regarding the Hawaiian lunar calendar, see the Appendix.)

Those born in Makali'i (late November to December) will have large families. If both the man and the woman were born in this month, their family will be even larger.

Those born in Ka'elo (late December to January) are highly affectionate toward their spouses and families. These men and women are charitable and enjoy many friendships. Their friends are showered with affection by the man or woman born in Ka'elo.

189

Those born in Kau-ula (late January to February), a time of violent storms, make mighty warriors in battle and will be victorious in all pursuits. They have short tempers.

Those born in Nana (late February to March) are confident and will succeed in whatever profession is chosen: farming, fishing, *kapa* beating, and so on. A highly auspicious month in which to be born.

Those born in Welo (late March to April) will be highly skilled at divination and counselling. "Illustrious" is the term to be applied to such persons, and their children will follow them in their profession with great success.

Those born in Ikiiki (late April to May) are fond of agriculture. Their houses will always be open to strangers and friends, but their families will enjoy the bulk of their affection.

Those born in Ka'aona (Late May to June) are fortunate, for they will be a favorite of chiefs and, if male, greatly desired by women. Such persons are known as "the intoxicating shrub of makalei" (a plant used to stupify fish).

Those born in Hina-ia-eleele (Late June to July) are lazy and ignorant, desiring only pleasurable activities. Learning is avoided by such persons.

Those born in Mahoe-mua (Late July to August) and Mahoe-hope (Late August to September) have come into this world during the "twin months," and are enigmas. They can be either good or evil. If their first act is evil, they will continue to be evil throughout their lives. If the first conscious action is good, they shall be good. If the first is good and the second evil, evil shall be their path. Such persons are fond of agriculture and fishing.

Those born in Ikuwa (Late September to October) possess extremely loud voices, which makes them perfect heralds for the chiefs. These men may become chiefs. Their opinions will be akin to the sound of thunder during the month of Ikuwa.

Those born in Welehu (Late October to November) shall be greatly fertile and will have many children. This is a highly auspicious month.

At least some of these predictions were based on the nature of the month in which the child was born: stormy months produce emotionally explosive children. Many other factors were also involved.

After the month had been noted, the specific day was taken into consideration. It should be noted that the Hawaiian "day" began at night; i.e., sunset marked the beginning of a new day, not sunrise. This is common among peoples that observe lunar calendars, since the moon, not the sun, is the revealer of the date. Sadly, birth omen information is incomplete; omens for only 20 of the 30 lunar days have been recorded. They follow here:

1. **Hilo:** No recorded traditions.

2. **Hoaka:** Men born on this day will grumble about everything, will make trouble, be stingy, unmerciful, and conceited. They will be clever at getting their way. Still, they will have some lovable qualities and will be quite efficient. Women will "show their teeth" (i.e., be angry), but will conceal their anger with affability. Dignified and unassuming will be used to describe them, but such women are truly hypocrites and vain. They often wait at the doors of others for free meals.

3. **Ku kahi:** Men are dauntless, strong of body, quite brave, unyielding and kind-hearted, though they constantly make mistakes. Women are "ensnarers," have little pride, and constantly eat food left over from the meals of others.

4. **Ku lua:** No traditions are available.

5. **Ku kolu:** No traditions are available.

6. **Ku pau:** A man born on this day will cling to all that he is taught. Properly taught as a boy, he will be a fine man. Taught evil, he will be quite evil. Nothing or no person can alter the character of a person born on this day. Women born on Ku pau are quite virtuous. They are good workers and are ashamed to ask for favors or to go to the homes of others. They will make female enemies without cause but will work hard and have prosperous, handsome men pursuing them.

7. **'Ole ku kahi:** These men are secretive about their prosperity and will hide it from others. They will gain little, depending unashamedly on women to support them; be lazy, gluttonous, fond of pleasurable activities, and hard-hearted. He will happily steal food from the gardens of women and children, or linger at the doors of others at mealtimes (so that he will be fed). Shamelessly, he'll send children to other houses to beg for food and other things, and will expect to be paid (in food) for caring for children. They are hard-hearted. Women born on this day will be virtuous and work hard with their hands, yet they'll also be quick-tempered and will often grumble. They'll also force others to work. (As is obvious, this is a ill-omened day for the birth of children—and just about everything else.)

8. **'Ole ku lua:** Men born on this day will be fond of pleasure but also apply themselves to work with zest. Women born on this day will be bad-tempered, talkative gossipers, fond of praise, and ready to assume honors that don't belong to them. They will enjoy associating with the *ali'i* (chiefs), do only a bit of work, and will be widely criticized by other women.

9. **'Ole ku kolu:** Men and women born on this day are quite acquisitive, merciless, and stingy. Everything that they possess will be gained from others.

10. **'Ole pau:** Men and women born on this day will enjoy great prosperity.

11. **Huna:** Men born on this day will be kind, modest, and hospitable, full of wisdom. They will also have enemies that speak out against them. They will be despised and troubled by others. Women will share these virtues with men, and their names will become famous.

12. **Mohalu:** Men or women born on this day will be skeptical but excellent workers. Women born on Mohalu will be lazy at work.

13. **Hua:** Men born on this day will be prosperous, greatly loved, and kindhearted. They will enjoy a famous name. Women will

also be prosperous, but won't attain a famous name or be greatly loved.

14. **Akua:** A man or woman born on this day will be prosperous, but will care nothing for his or her parents. "Bad-hearted" describes these people, who will disgrace their families and give away all of their possessions. However, a man or woman born during the daylight hours on Akua will love everyone.

15. **Hoku:** Men and woman born on this day will be famous and prosperous. However, they'll also have many enemies. Women will be quite active.

16. **Mahealani:** Men or women born on this day will be "strivers." This is a highly auspicious day.

17. **Kulu:** A man or woman born on this day will be prosperous, affectionate, and greatly loved by all.

18. **La'au ku kahi:** Men and women born on this day will be fine of character. They're eager for knowledge and want to learn and hear new things.

19. **La'au ku lua:** See La'au ku kahi.

20. **La'au pau:** No information is available.

21. **'Ole ku kahi:** Men and women born on this day will be inefficient and ineffective.

22. **'Ole ku lua:** Men and women born on this day will be modest and quiet.

23. **'Ole pau:** No information is available.

24. **Kaloa ku kahi:** Persons born on this day will be good.

25. **Kaloa ku lua:** This is an auspicious day upon which to be born.

26. **Kaloa pau:** No information is available.

27. **Kane:** No information is available.

28. **Lono:** No information is available.

29. **Mauli:** No information is available.

30. **Muku:** No information is available.

Even this fragmentary list of "day" birth omens reveals much. Though Hawaiians had no concept of the zodiac, and indeed saw different constellations than we do, they still relied on the moon and stars to determine future character. The importance placed upon such omens can't today be determined.

Hawaiians were quite logical in assuming that humans would be affected by the night of the moon upon which they had been born. Didn't the moon date affect storms, the sea (tides), and fish? Didn't bananas planted on certain nights grow longer and more flavorful? Such observations naturally led to the conclusion that the moon also affected human behavior.

CHAPTER TWENTY-ONE

Contemporary Survival of Traditional Hawaiian Spirituality

In this book we've surveyed some aspects of ancient Hawaiian religious and magical practice. I've generally written of these in the past tense, as if traditional Hawaiian spirituality had completely died out.

But are the old ways gone? Have the deities survived the onslaught of Western (and Eastern) religion, technology, and ideals? Ask the elderly Hawaiian woman who ritually bathes in the sea for purification *(kapu kai)*. Ask the fisherman who won't take bananas on his boat, or the children who refuse to play in haunted woods.

Ask those who throw offerings into lava flows while asking Pele to spare their houses from fiery destruction. Ask the farmers who still pray to Lono for fine weather and good crops. Ask persons who've seen the Night Marchers, or who have given a ride to a beautiful young woman who suddenly vanished without a trace from their cars.

Why do people still avoid taking pork over the Pali (on Oahu) or on the Saddle Road (on the Big Island)? Why do *ki* plants still surround and protect homes? Why do nominal Christians still call upon relative *kahuna* to treat minor ailments with both non-Christian prayer and herbal remedies? Why do Hawaiians still leave offerings (also known as "blessings") of *ki*-leaf wrapped rocks at temples?

The answers to these questions is plain: The strong spiritual undercurrent of old Hawai'i is still alive. Those that live on the sacred land are touched by its *mana*. Many Protestants, Catholics, Buddhists, Mormons, and members of other religions are unable to still their ears to the joyous spiritual melodies that their families have sung for generations.

Traditional Hawaiian spirituality was practiced for over 500 years. Christianity and other religions have made their mark in Hawai'i only in the last 180 years. Despite the wishes of zealous missionaries, deeply ingrained religious truths are difficult to set aside, and seeds of the old ways continue to be passed from generation to generation.

Though the outer forms of this religious expression have been greatly changed, the inner connections with the land, the *akua*, and *'aumakua* are still felt, and these impel some persons toward ritual activity.

Some Hawaiians will dislike these words. "We've put all that superstition behind us," they'll state. "We've known the true god for a long time now." But when even Christian ministers bless construction sites with salt water and a *ki* leaf, the old ways haven't been completely forgotten.

Most outward expressions of traditional Hawaiian spirituality are performed in secret within the home, on lonely beaches, in forests, and at isolated temples. Some examples of these are *pi kai* (sprinkling with salt and water for purification, exorcism of spirits, and protection), *kapu kai* (ritual sea bathing), religious *hula,* offering the fruits of fishing or the fields on small shrines, avoiding eating certain foods due to *'aumakua* links, and reverencing places and old *pohaku* (stones).

Most of these contemporary expressions of traditional Hawaiian spirituality are prayers: to the *'aumakua* and the *akua* every morning

Traditional offerings continue at the City of Refuge, Hawai'i.

and evening, to the *'aumakua* for forgiveness, to the *akua* when gathering flowers and plants for medicine or ornament, to Ku for protection, Lono for fertile fields, Kane for healing, Laka for proficiency at *hula,* Haumea for easy childbirth, Ku'ula for abundant fish, and Kanaloa for safe sailing.

Many persons continue to experience glimpses of the psychic world that still whispers in Hawai'i: visions of Pele and other deities, prophetic dreams from the *'aumakua,* hearing voices or seeing deceased relatives, examining omens plainly laid before them. These may even occur to cultural Hawaiians who express little or no interest in their people's traditional spirituality.

Many adult Hawaiians with whom I've spoken are quite familiar with the *akua* and with their religious heritage. I've received complex details of traditional Hawaiian spirituality from persons who had never opened a book or attended a class on the subject. This lore is simply common knowledge in some families. Though such persons might say, "Ku was once worshipped," the fact is that Ku is still worshipped—it simply isn't discussed.

Other Hawaiians are quite unabashed about their spiritual beliefs, and openly state "I pray to Ku," or "Of course Pele's real. No one who's been to a lava flow or an eruption can doubt Her physical and spiritual presence." Such persons are rare, but their number are growing as new generations of young cultural Hawaiians discover their spiritual heritage.

Within the family unit, *ho'oponopono* is still in frequent use. This is a prayerful family conference designed to discuss problems, find their root causes, solve them, and forgive all concerned. In pre-missionary times, this included lengthy prayers to the *akua* and *'aumakua*. Though today only Akua (the Christian "God") may be invoked, the structure of this meeting is clearly pre-Christian, and is but one example of the inherent value of traditional Hawaiian culture.

Religion is an expression of spirituality. All religions are alike, in that they're designed to give their followers spiritually satisfying experiences and belief systems. Though religions and sects have differing ideas concerning the nature of deity and the "correct" modes of worship, all share this similar goal. This was also true of the ancient Hawaiians.

This religion, borne of fertile land, fresh water, abundant rain, bounteous oceans, spectacular volcanoes, and dazzling skies, will never die. Though today the sacred drums rarely echo from temples, present-day cultural Hawaiians have eagerly grasped many of the remaining traces of traditional belief and thought, and with them, are preserving remnants of their spiritual heritage. Just as the man-god Maui pulled up the islands of Hawai'i from the bottom of the sea with his magic fishhook, so too are many contemporary Hawaiians struggling to preserve elements of their traditional spirituality from total extinction.

How many see Hina in the moon? Haloa in *poi?* Ku'ula in the fish that splash in the ocean? Such questions can't be answered, save by the Hawaiians themselves.

One thing is clear, however: traditional Hawaiian spirituality has survived.

The Hawaiian Lunar Calendar

Like many other peoples, the Hawaiians governed time by means of a lunar calendar; i.e., one based upon the 29½-day lunar cycle. Though the basic structure of this calendar was universal in old Hawai'i, the names for each night (the days began at sunset) varied considerably, even on the same island.

Hawai'i recognized two seasons: dry and wet. Kau was the time of great heat and dryness on the islands. Summer usually began in early May, just when the Pleiades set as the sun rises. Ho'oilo (our winter) began in October, when the weather turned cool and wet.

Dividing these two seasons were the 12 lunar months. Once again, there was great diversity in naming the months and of the activities appropriate to them. On the island of Hawai'i, the months were named as follows:

Kaelo (roughly corresponds with our January)
Kau-lua (February)
Nana (March)
Welo (April)

Ikiiki (May)
Kaaona (June)
Hina-ia-eleele (July)
Mahoe-mua (August)
Mahoe-hope (September)
Ikuwa (October)
Welehu (November)
Makalii (December)

The lunar calendar was an important part of the spiritual lives of the Hawaiians. Save for the Makahiki and a few other rites, Hawaiians lacked yearly rituals. In their place they observed monthly rites of worship, putting aside work in favor of prayer. The lunar calendar also governed fishing, agriculture, and many other facets of human life.

The Hawaiians seemed to know what farmers everywhere have known—that the phases of the moon have a direct influence on plants. The lunar calendar is thus also a type of farmer's almanac. It governed fishing, *kapa* making, and prayer as well.

Following is a typical Hawaiian lunar calendar. Some variations in name and purpose for each day also exist. Information is sketchy.

1. **Hilo:** This is the night of the new moon and the first night of the *kapu* period of Ku during which his worshippers performed various rites. Generally, this is a bad day for healing.

2. **Hoaka:** A bad night for fishing, for ghosts cast shadows and frighten away fish. The second night of the Ku *kapu*. The *akua* could also be persuaded to "cast their shadows" on their worshippers. Excellent for healing.

3. **Ku kahi:** Ku *kapu* ends.

4. **Ku lua:** Kalo planted will have two shoots.

5. **Ku kolu:** Low tides are ideal for gathering *limu* (seaweed).

6. **Ku pau:** Little information is available.

7. **'Ole ku kahi:** Considered unfortunate for planting and much of anything else, including fishing. The seas are rough. *Kahuna lapa'au* might wait to begin healings until after these 'ole nights were passed.

8. **'Ole ku lua:** See 'Ole ku kahi.

9. **'Ole ku kolu:** See 'Ole ku kahi.

10. **'Ole pau:** End of the 'ole nights.

11. **Huna:** Recommended for planting root plants and gourds. Good fishing.

12. **Mohalu:** Sacred to Lono, *akua* of vegetation. Fish, fruits, and seaweed are *kapu* to eat. Flowers planted on this night will be as round and perfect as the moon.

13. **Hua:** Sacred night of Lono. Good fishing; the land is fruitful.

14. **Akua:** A night generally *kapu* to all the *akua*. Offerings are made to increase food. One of the nights when the ghostly processions of the Night Marchers are commonly seen. (See Chapter 16.)

15. **Hoku:** If planted on Hoku, root plants and bananas will be prolific, though small-fruited. Good fishing.

16. **Mahealani:** Night of the full moon. Good for all work. Fertility of all plants. "Luck." A good night during which to divine the future or to ask for omens from the *akua* to find hidden objects.

17. **Kulu:** A time for offering the first fruits to the *akua*.

18. **La'au ku kahi:** A day favored for gathering medicinal plants and for creating medicines.

19. **La'au ku lua:** See La'au ku kahi.

20. **La'au pau:** A good day for planting. See La'au ku kahi.

21. **'Ole ku kahi:** Not recommended for fishing, planting, or much of anything else. Not good for healing.

22. **'Ole ku lua:** See 'Ole ku kahi.

23. **'Ole pau:** First *kapu* day of Kanaloa. Offerings and sacrifice (not human) are made, and prayers said. Good for healing.

24. **Kaloa ku kahi:** Second *kapu* day of Kanaloa. Offerings and prayers. Healing.

25. **Kaloa ku lua:** Good for planting plants with long stems (such as bananas, *hala,* sugar cane, bamboo). Good for healing.

26. **Kaloa pau:** End of Kanaloa *kapu* period.

27. **Kane:** Sacred to the *akua* after which it is named. Prayers are made to Kane and Lono. No planting or fishing is allowed—such activities were *kapu*. No fires are made, no *kapa* is beaten, and all sound is forbidden. Another night on which the Night Marchers, ghosts, and spirits are often seen. Good for healing. Families who recognized sharks as *'aumakua* might choose this day to transfigure their recently deceased relatives into sharks.

28. **Lono:** Second day of Kane *kapu*. Prayers for rain were made. Gourds planted at this time were fruitful (gourds were a *kino lau* of Lono). Good for healing and all positive things. Sound *kapu* again in effect.

29. **Mauli:** A good day for marriage. Fishing good. Tides are low.

30. **Muku:** The moon vanishes *(muku)*. Fishing is good, but healing *kahuna* shouldn't begin treating patients on this night, as the name also means "cut-off," which is inauspicious.

Obviously, a calendar of this type isn't astronomically correct. The night of Hilo had to fall on the new moon; Mahealani on the full. Therefore, one day had to be deleted at regular intervals. When this was necessary, one night was simply dropped from the month. Such periodic corrections are necessary with any lunar calendar. Astronomical knowledge, gathered and stored in the minds of *kahuna*, was responsible for the creation of Hawai'i's calendar.

Ritual Periods

As can be seen by the above, there were four *kapu* periods each month:

  1st, 2nd, and 3rd days were sacred to Ku
  12th and 13th days were sacred to Lono
  23rd and 24th days were sacred to Kanaloa
  27th and 28th days were sacred to Kane

Thus, there was a *kapu* period about every week. During these times, only those who prayed to these deities observed their *kapu*. This usually meant that they didn't work or play, avoided eating certain foods, and prayed and gave offerings to their deities. Such *kapu* weren't universally recognized since there wasn't one religious structure, but were rigorously kept by those who were impelled to do so.

This was the case for about eight months each year. However, during the yearly four-month long Makahiki festival, these ritual periods weren't observed. People were "freed" from the *kapu* during the Makahiki, when all attention was turned toward making offerings to Lono, rituals, and sports competitions. (When Hawaiians became Christians, Sunday became the only *kapu* day, as it was "sacred" to the new god.)

Hawaiian Glossary

This glossary of Hawaiian words and phrases isn't by any means complete or authoritative. See *Hawaiian Dictionary* by Mary Kawena Pukui and Samuel L. Elbert for more information.

At first I hesitated using many of these words in this book, because most persons are unfamiliar with the Hawaiian language. However, it soon became apparent that this was impossible: many Hawaiian words have no exact equivalent in English. Even when they can be translated, two or three words are usually necessary.

'A'a: Crumbly, harsh lava (compare with **pahoehoe**).

'Aha'aina: A feast; literally, a "meal gathering." Today usually termed **luau.**

'Aina: Land, the earth; the soil.

Akaku: Visions or waking dreams, usually of a warning nature.

Akua: God, goddess; deity, deities. In the Christian era, "Akua" was used to refer to the Christian god.

Akualele: Flying gods or spirits sent to bring destruction on enemies.

'Alaea: Red, water-soluble earth, used to color salt (to be used as a condiment), for dyeing, and in medicine. ("Red salt" is today usually known as **'alae,** though anciently this referred to the mudhen, a black wading bird.)

Ali'i: The chiefly class of old Hawai'i.

'Ana 'ana: Black magic; sorcery. **Kahuna 'ana 'ana** caused death through ritual on order from the ruling **ali'i.**

'Anai: To curse; a curse.

'Apu: A cup.

'Aumakua: Deified ancestral spirits worshipped within a family framework.

'Awa: A plant *(Piper methysticum)* whose roots are used to create an intoxicating drink; also the drink itself.

'Ele 'ele: The color black.

Haka: A medium; one who willingly allows a spirit or **akua** to possess him or her to reveal information to the family.

Hale o Papa: "House of (the goddess) Papa," a separate structure outside of **heiau** in which female chiefs worshipped.

Hale pea: A menstrual house, in which women stayed during their menstruation.

Haole: Foreign, foreigner. Today usually used in reference to caucasians.

Hana aloha: Literally, "love work." Magic directed toward creating or strenthening love, performed by **kahuna aloha.**

Heiau: Temple; shrine; a place where offerings are made to the **akua.** A permanent or temporary center of group religious ceremony.

Heiau ho'oulu 'ai: Temple to increase fertility of the land and abundance of crops.

Heiau ho'oulu ua: A temple in which prayers for rain were made.

Heiau kalua ua: A temple for halting rains.

Heiau ma'o: A small temporary temple created for increasing food production.

Ho'ailona: An omen, sign, or predictive event.

Ho'ounauna: The practice of sending spirits on positive or destructive missions.

Ho'okalakupua: Magic; wondrous actions.

Hula: Dance in old Hawai'i, specifically that which commemorated famous individuals, **akua,** or places. Its dancers worshipped Laka, Pele, and other deities.

Huna: Small, little, a speck; secret or hidden. The eleventh night of the Hawaiian lunar calendar. On the mainland today, the word is often used to refer to Max Freedom Long's system of quasi-Hawaiian psychological magic. In old Hawai'i, no one practiced **huna.**

Ike papalua: Psychic awareness. An unusually rare gift in old Hawaiian culture.

Ipu: A gourd; a gourd container. Used for storing feather garments, water, and food, among other things, and for making rat guards on the legs of offering stands in temples. Also used during divination.

Ipu 'olelo: A gourd used in divination. Literally, "speaking gourd."

Kahiki: The traditional homeland of the Hawaiians, from where they launched their double canoes on their voyages of discovery. Probably Tahiti or one of the other Society Islands.

Kahu: A "keeper" of a specific god, goddess, or spirit; a person with a profound relationship with deity. A **kahu** of Pele is one example; they were priests (or priestesses) but usually didn't perform public rituals.

Ka huaka'i o ka po: The Night Marchers; processions of dead chiefs, chiefesses, and gods who walk at night in ghostly splendor. To be seen by them was certain death.

Kahuna: Expert in any of several professions. Popularly associated with sorcery, all were indeed priests or priestesses, since all professions were guided by specific deities, but most weren't sorcerers. **Kahuna** does not mean "keeper of the secret."

Kahuna aloha: Expert in love magic.

Kahuna 'ana 'ana: An expert in sorcery, including the act of "praying to death."

Kahuna haha: An expert in diagnosis.

Kahuna ha'iha'i iwi: A bone-setting expert.

Kahuna ho'ohanau: An expert at midwivery.

Kahuna ho'ohapai keiki: A medical expert who ritually induced pregnancy.

Kahuna ho'okelewa'a: An expert nagivator.

Kahuna ho'opi'opi'po: An expert in causing sickness or distress by concentration and gesture.

Kahuna ho'oulu 'ai: An agricultural expert.

Kahuna kalai: Expert carver.

Kahuna kalai wa'a: Expert canoe carver.

Kahuna kuni: Expert anti-sorcerer who destroyed those **kahuna 'ana 'ana** who abused their sorcerous activities.

Kahuna la'au lapa'au: Herbal doctor.

Kahuna kilo kilo: An expert who observed the skies for omens.

Kahuna kuhikuhi pu'uone: Architects; experts who selected sites for the erection of temples, fishponds, and homes.

Kahuna lomilomi: An expert massage technician.

Kahuna nana uli: Weather prophet.

Kahuna nui: Counsellor to the chiefs; a specialized function of the **kahuna po'o** class.

Kahuna po'o: High priest; expert in all arts.

Kahuna pule: "Prayer expert" who prayed within the **heiau**.

Kahuna pule wahine: Female prayer experts who were allowed into the **heiau**, which was usually **kapu** to women.

Kalo *(Colocasia esculentum):* The food staple of old Hawai'i. Today usually pronounced "taro."

Kanawai: A law, rule, statute, decree, usually stated by **ali'i.**

Kapa: Cloth made from the bark of the **wauke** and other trees. Hawaiians lacked knowledge of spinning.

Kapu: A code of religious and civil laws that governed behaviour in old Hawai'i. Breaking a **kapu** could result in the punishment of death. The system was overthrown in 1819.

Kapu kai: A ceremonial sea bath used for purification, especially by patients after healing regimens or following contact with defiling substances.

Kaula: A prophet; one who speaks of future events.

Kaula wahine: A woman prophet; a priestess.

Kauwa: The "untouchable" class of old Hawai'i; slaves.

Kea: The color white.

Ki: A plant *(Dracaena terminalis)* that was utilized in numerous ways in old Hawai'i. Today usually pronounced "ti."

Ki'i: Representations of the gods, goddesses, and **'aumakua** fashioned of wood, stone, feathers, and other materials. Often pronounced "tiki."

Kino lau: The "many bodies" (plant, animal, human, stone, fish, bird, wind, cloud, etc.) that the **akua** and **'aumakua** could assume at will.

Ko'a: Fishing shrines set beside the sea or freshwater rivers for abundant catches.

Kuahu: Altar.

Kuni: Literally, "to burn." A ritual by which a sorcerer who has cursed others is destroyed. Part of the ritual involved burning something that belongs to the offending sorcerer.

Kupua: Nature spirits; demi-deities; spiritual beings that are less than divine but more than human.

Lapu: Ghost.

Lauhala: The leaves of the **hala** *(Pandanus odoratissimus)*.

Lei: A garland worn around the neck, wrists, ankles, or on the head. **Lei** were also used as offerings to the gods. They were made of seeds, fruits, flowers, leaves, ferns, seaweed, shells, feathers, and human hair.

Leina: The "leaping place" where spirit/souls of the dead jump from the earth into the underworld. Each island had at least one such place.

Lele: A stand upon which offerings were placed in temples. The word means "to fly;" offerings placed here would fly to the **akua**.

Limu: A general term for all plants that live in the ocean; seaweed.

Luakini: Human sacrifice **heiau**, traditionally introduced in Hawai'i in the twelfth century.

Lua 'uhane: The "spirit pit" at the inner corner of the eye through which the **'uhane** (spirit) left at night to wander, and through which it returned in the morning.

Luau: The young leaves of the kalo cooked with coconut milk and octopus or chicken. The use of this food's name for Hawaiian feasts dates back no earlier than 1856. The original term for feasts was **'aha'aina.**

Mai'a: Banana.

Maka'aina: The common people of old Hawai'i.

Malo: A loincloth created of barkcloth and worn by all men in Hawai'i.

Mana: Spiritual power possessed in vast amounts by the gods, goddesses, and family ancestral spirits; in lesser quantity by humans. One use of **mana** is the practice of magic.

Maunu: "Bait" (hair, spittle, nail parings, clothing) used in sorcerous activities to afflict the original owner.

Mapele: A peaceful temple, dedicated to agriculture, rain-bringing, and other positive ends. Usually dedicated to Lono.

Melemele: The color yellow.

Menehune: A legendary race of small people who performed construction jobs throughout the islands. May have been a people who migrated to Hawai'i at an early period and were encountered by later migrants. Now relegated to the realm of folklore.

Moe 'uhane: Dreams, an important source of information. It was through dreams that the **'aumakua** often communicated with their living descendants.

Moha'i: Sacrifice of fruits, vegetables, bark cloth, dogs, pigs, **'awa,** and humans. Sacrifice was an integral part of traditional Hawaiian spirituality. The **akua** ate the essence of the food; humans usually later consumed the physical forms (save, in rare occasions, human sacrifices).

Ohana: Family; the most important social unit in old Hawai'i.

'Olelo: Speech; words; language; utterances.

'Olena. Turmeric *(Curcurma domestica),* widely used in food preparation, medicine, and dyeing. Also used in the creation of purifying waters.

'O'o; 'O'o 'a'a: A small black bird with tufts of yellow feathers under the wings. Now extinct.

'Opihi: A limpet *(Cellana* spp.) that thrives on wave-splashed rocks. Relished as source of food, some families recognized the **'opihi** as an **'aumakua** and avoided its ingestion.

Pi kai: A ritual purification performed by sprinkling sea water or salted water, generally with a **ki** leaf.

Pi kai 'olena: Sprinkling with sea water or salted water mixed with 'olena root for purificatory purposes.

Pi kai kea: To sprinkle with "white" water; i.e., that gathered from foamy (and thus white-appearing) sea waves.

Po: The realm of darkness; the eternal sea; the place where the dead and 'aumakua dwell. Also night; obscurity.

Pohaku: Stones. Stones were of vital importance in old Hawai'i.

Pohaku hanau: Stones to which **ali'i** women in labor would journey to give birth.

Pule: Prayer. Direction communication with the deities and the 'aumakua; the commonest form of religious expression. Prayer was a vehicle of moving **mana.**

Pu'uhonua: A place of refuge to which the **kapu** breaker or defeated soldier could retire in safety and be guarded and purified by the attendant priests. At least one existed in every district on every inhabited island.

'Uala: The sweet potato *(Ipomoea batatas),* one of the standard foods in Hawai'i. Women often cultivated it whereas other food plants were the sole province of men.

'Uhane: The spirit, soul, and animating force of humans. In some usages, a ghost.

'Ula; 'Ulaula: The color red.

Ulalelo: Voices giving warning heard during the day from deceased relatives.

Umeke: A wooden bowl. Known today as a calabash.

'Unihipili: The trapped spirit/soul of a deceased loved one, sent on missions of mercy or errands of destruction by its keeper. An artificially detained and maintained ghost.

Waʻa: Canoe.

Wai: Water, of great importance in Hawaiian religion. There were many types: rain water, spring water, river water, ocean water, "white" ocean water (the foam on the tops of waves, caught in gourds). Each had specific religio-magical uses.

Wai huikala: Water of purification, either sea water or fresh water mixed with salt and other substances, including ʻolena and **limu.**

Waihoʻoluʻu: Color; hues.

Bibliography

Abbott, Isabella Aiona, *Limu: An Ethnobotanical Study of Some Hawaiian Seaweeds*. Lawai (Kaua'i, Hawai'i): Pacific Tropical Botanical Gardens, 1984.

Seaweed in old Hawai'i: its lore, uses, and diversity. A remarkable, though short, survey of this often overlooked source of nourishment and medicine.

Abbot, Isabella Aiona, *La'au Hawai'i: Traditional Hawaiian Uses of Plants*. Honolulu: Bishop Museum Press, 1992.

A well-documented account of the myriad of uses that the Hawaiians had for plants. Fully illustrated.

Anonymous, *Hawaii's Birds*. Honolulu: Hawai'i Audubon Society, 1989.

An introduction to both endemic and introduced Hawaiian birds, with full-color photographs.

Ariyoshi, Rita, "Kahuna: The Keepers of the Secrets" in *Pleasant Hawaii*, Vol. 3, No. 4; Summer 1990.

A revealing article concerning this topic.

Baldwin, Charles W., *Geography of the Hawaiian Islands*. New York: American Book Company, 1908.

Wonderful early photographs of Hawai'i and charming descriptions of time long past.

Barrere, Dorothy B., Mary Kawena Pukui, Marion Kelly, *Hula: Historical Perspectives*. Pacific Anthropological Records #30. Honolulu: Department of Anthropology, Bishop Museum, 1980.

A detailed account of *hula,* this work explores many common misconceptions concerning the dance. A classic.

Beckwith, Martha, *Hawaiian Mythology.* Honolulu: University Press of Hawaii, 1970.

A monumental survey of Hawaiian legends and spirituality.

Beckwith, Martha (translator, editor, and commentator), *The Kumulipo: A Hawaiian Creation Chant.* Chicago: The University of Chicago Press, 1951.

An in-depth study of the most famous of geneological chants, by which early Hawaiians recorded their history.

Bowman, Pierre, "Mookini Luakini: Easing the Kapu for Today's Needs." *Honolulu Advertiser,* Tuesday, May 4, 1982.

An interview with Momi Mookini Lum, whose family has always been *kahuna* of Mo'okini Heiau on the island of Hawai'i. A fascinating story.

Burrows, Edwin G., *Western Polynesia: A Study of Cultural Differentiation.* Dunedin (New Zealand): University Book Shop Ltd., 1970.

Interesting background information on Polynesian ways.

Charlot, John, *The Kamapua'a Literature: The Classical Traditions of the Hawaiian Pig God as a Body of Literature.* La'ie (Hawai'i): The Institute for Polynesian Studies, Brigham Young University, 1987.

Much information regarding Kamapua'a.

Chun, Malcolm Naea (translator), *Hawaiian Medicine Book: He Buke Laau Lapaau.* Honolulu: The Bess Press, 1986.

An account of healing in old Hawai'i.

Cox, J. Halley and William H. Davenport, *Hawaiian Sculpture*. Honolulu: The University Press of Hawaii, 1974.

Survey of all extant wooden sculptures from old Hawai'i, most of which are of of *akua* or *'aumakua*.

Culliney, John L., *Islands in a Far Sea: Nature and Man in Hawaii*. San Francisco: Sierra Club Books, 1988.

A cautionary look at the continuing destruction of the Hawaiian ecosystem.

de Fries, Emma, "Malo-Clad Warriors Scare off Workers." *The Honolulu Sunday Star-Bulletin,* October 31, 1971.

Degener, Otto, *Plants of Hawaii National Part Illustrative of Plants and Customs of the South Seas.* 1930. Reprinted Ann Arbor: Braun-Brumfield Inc., 1975.

Plants of old Hawai'i.

Dickey, Lyle A., *String Figures from Hawaii*. Honolulu: Bishop Museum, 1928. Reprinted Millwood (New York): Kraus Reprint, 1985.

String figures used in healing and magic.

Dudley, Michael Kioni, *Man, Gods and Nature: A Hawaiian Nation I*. Honolulu: Na Kane O Ka Malo Press, 1990.

An in-depth, mystical look at traditional Hawaiian spiritual and cultural values. A unique book.

Ellis, *Polynesian Researches: Hawaii*. 1842. Reprinted Rutland (Vermont): Charles E. Tuttle, 1974.

An early account of *hula*. Much information regarding Laka and Pele.

Fornander, Abraham, *An Account of the Polynesian Race: Its Origins and Migrations.* 1877. Reprinted Rutland (Vermont): Charles E. Tuttle, 1969.

Three volumes bound as one. A massive work filled with traditional Hawaiian cultural information: sacred stories, omens, religion, genealogies, and much more.

Frierson, Pamela, *The Burning Island: A Journey through Myth and History in Volcano Country, Hawai'i.*

Major sections are devoted to Pele and her family.

Gutmanis, June, *Kahuna La'au Lapa'au: The Practice of Hawaiian Herbal Medicine.* Honolulu: Island Heritage Unlimited, 1979.

Wonderful account of healing in old Hawai'i. Beautiful full-color paintings of plants.

Gutmanis, June, *Na Pule Kahiko: Ancient Hawaiian Prayers.* Honolulu: Editions Limited, 1983.

Old prayers for every occasion, from launching a canoe to whipping up winds for kite flying.

Gutmanis, June, *Pohaku: Hawaiian Stones.* Laie (O'ahu): Brigham Young University—Hawaii Campus, N.D.

A remarkable look at the importance of stones to early Hawaiians, with stories of some of the most famous examples.

Handy, E. S. Craighill (and others), *Ancient Hawaiian Civilization: A Series of Lectures Delivered at The Kamehameha Schools.* 1933. Reprinted Rutland, Vermont: Charles E. Tuttle, 1965.

Fascinating collection of lectures on a variety of topics, including religion, agriculture, astronomy, medicine, and warfare.

Handy, E. S. Craighill, Elizabeth Green Handy, and Mary Kawena Pukui, *Native Planters in Old Hawaii: Their Life, Lore and Environment.* Honolulu: Bishop Museum Press, 1972.

An exhaustive account of plants and animals in old Hawai'i. Spiritual connections with plants are thoroughly described.

Handy, E. S. Craighill and Mary Kawena Pukui, *The Polynesian Family System in Ka-'u, Hawaii'.* 1958. Reprinted Rutland (Vermont): Charles E. Tuttle, 1972.

An engrossing study of social customs, religion, medicine, and spirit work in old Hawai'i.

Hazlett, Richard W., *Pu'uhonua O Honaunau: Place of Refuge.* Hawai'i Natural History Association/The National Park Service, 1986.

A fine book, geared toward younger readers, with much information concerning life in ancient Hawai'i. Heavily illustrated with line drawings.

Hildebrandt, William, *Flora of the Hawaiian Islands.* 1888. Reprinted New York: Hafner, 1965.

Invaluable for plant identification.

Hiroa, Te Rangi (Peter S. Buck), *Arts and Crafts of Hawaii: Section XI: Religion.* 1957. Reprinted (in separate sections) Honolulu: Bishop Museum Press, 1964.

Fascinating account of *heiau,* images of the deities, offerings, and shrines.

Hiroa, Te Rangi (Peter S. Buck), *Arts and Crafts of Hawaii: Section XII: Ornaments (Personal Adornment).* 1957. Reprinted (in separate sections) Honolulu: Bishop Museum Press, 1964.

Lei made of both perishable and non-perishable materials.

Hoyt, Helen P., *The Night Marchers: A Tale of the Huaka'i Po.* Honolulu/Norfolk Island (Australia): Island Heritage, 1976.

A lavishly produced, limited edition book recounting a tale told to the author by an aged Hawaiian concerning the night marchers. A "Further Reading" section includes essays concerning the night marchers as well as articles about ghosts. An enchanting book.

Kane, Herb Kawainui, *Pele: Goddes of Hawai'i's Volcanoes.* Captain Cook (Hawai'i): The Kawainui Press, 1987.

A beautifully illustrated account of Pele by the celebrated artist, with personal notes.

Kelly, Marion, *Pele and Hi'iaka.* Honolulu: Bernice P. Bishop Museum, 1984.

A charming retelling of some of their adventures.

Ii, John Papa, *Fragments of Hawaiian History.* Mary Kawena Pukui, translator. Honolulu: Bishop Museum, 1983.

Memoirs of a man whose father was an attendant to Kamehameha I. A fascinating look at early life in Hawai'i, including healing practices, religious rituals, and other topics of immense interest.

Judd, Henry P., *The Hawaiian Language.* Honolulu: Hawaiian Service, 1939.

A short guide to the language, with reading selections and a dictionary.

Kaaiakamanu, D. M., and J. K. Akina, *Hawaiian Herbs of Medicinal Value*. Akaiko Akana, translator. 1922. Reprinted Honolulu/Rutland (Vermont); Pacific Book House/Charles E. Tuttle: N.D.

A curious collection of medicinal uses of Hawaiian plants. Definitely not for use by the inexperienced.

Kalakaua, King David, *The Legends and Myths of Hawaii*. 1888. Reprinted Rutland (Vermont): Charles E. Tuttle, 1972.

A romantic collection of traditional stories retold by the "Merry Monarch" who did much to preserve what he could of the rapidly vanishing traditional Hawaiian culture. An introduction discusses Hawaiian history, *akua*, and *kapu*. A lively book written in Victorian prose.

Kamakau, Samuel Manaiakalani, *Ka Po'e Kahiko: The People of Old*. Mary Kawena Pukui, translator. Honolulu: Bishop Museum Press, 1964.

A collection of articles written between 1866 and 1871 regarding life in old Hawai'i. Much discussion of *'aumakua*, medicine, magic, and sorcery.

Kamakau, Samuel Manaiakalani, *Na Hana a ka Po'e Kahiko: The Works of the People of Old*. Mary Kawena Pukui, translator. Honolulu: Bishop Museum Press, 1976.

This collection of articles by the same author discusses crafts, fishing, agriculture, and *heiau*.

Kelly, Marion, "Some Problems with Early Descriptions of Hawaiian Culture" in *Polynesian Culture History: Essays in Honor of Kenneth P. Emory*. Genevieve A. Highland, editor. Honolulu: Bishop Museum Press, 1967.

A short essay concerning the undetected influence of Western culture in early accounts of Hawai'i.

Kennedy, Joseph, "Hawaiian Archaeology: The Pursuit of Antiquity in a Very Small Place." *Archaeology*, Volume 40, Number 5, September/October 1987.

Report of how the archaeological record of Hawai'i is being threatened by rapid development.

Kirch, Patrick Vinton, *Feathered Gods and Fishhooks: An Introduction to Hawaiian Archaeology and Prehistory.* Honolulu: University of Hawaii Press, 1985.

A ground-breaking look at Hawaiian prehistory according to archaelogical finds.

Krauss, Beatrice H., *Ethnobotany of the Hawaiians.* Harold L. Lyon Arboretum Lecture #5. Honolulu: Harold L. Lyon Arboretum, University of Hawaii, 1978.

This lecture includes a wide range of plant uses in traditional Hawaiian culture.

Krauss, Beatrice H., *Native Plants Used as Medicine in Hawaii.* Honolulu: Harold H. Lyon Arboretum, University of Hawaii, 1979.

A brief look at medicinal uses of plants past and present in Hawai'i.

Lamoureux, Charles H., *Trailside Plants of Hawaii's National Parks.* Volcano (Hawai'i): Hawaii Natural History Association, 1976.

Color photographs and expert description of some common Hawaiian plants. Ancient uses are included.

Lee, Pali Jae and Koko Willis, *Tales From the Night Rainbow: Mo'olelo o na Po Makole.* Honolulu: Night Rainbow Publishing, 1990.

This book presents an oral history of the Hawaiian people, aspects of their culture, and information concerning Moloka'i. Even the authors admit that much of the information contained within this book differs from most of what has been published. Nevertheless, they write that this is what they were taught. A luminous work.

Linnekin, Jocelyn, *Sacred Queens and Women of Consequence: Rank, Gender and Colonialism in the Hawaiian Islands.* Ann Arbor (Michigan): The University of Michigan Press, 1900.

An in-depth account of women's place in late pre-contact and early post-contact Hawai'i. The first two chapters, which discuss women's role in religion and the *kapu* system, are of the most interest to our subject.

Luomala, Katharine, *Voices on the Wind: Polynesian Myths and Chants.* Honolulu: Bishop Museum Press, 1955.

A cross-cultural survey of traditional Pacific spirituality, with special emphasis on Hawai'i.

Macdonald, Gordon A., and Agatin T. Abbott, *Volcanoes in the Sea.* Honolulu: The University Press of Hawaii, 1977.

A fascinating geological account of volcanic activity in Hawai'i. A revised edition has been printed.

Malo, David, *Moolelo Hawaii (Hawaiian Antiquities).* Nathaniel B. Emerson, translator. 1898. Reprinted Honolulu: Bishop Museum Press, 1971.

A unique account of early Hawai'i by a man born before the *kapu* system had been overthrown. Topics include religion, medicine, sorcery, *heiau*, food, and much else of interest.

McBride, L. R., *The Kahuna: Versatile Mystics of Old Hawaii.* Hilo (Hawai'i): Petroglyph Press, 1972.

A short account of these experts.

McBride, L. R., *Petroglyphs of Hawaii.* Hilo (Hawai'i): Petroglyph Press, 1969.

A short illustrated history.

McBride, L. R., *Practical Folk Medicine of Hawaii.* Hilo (Hawai'i): The Petroglyph Press, 1975.

A brief look at plants and their medicinal uses.

McDonald, Marie A., *Ka Lei: The Leis of Hawaii.* Honolulu and Waipahu: Topgallant/Press Pacifica, 1985.

A glorious full-color survey of ancient and modern *lei*. Much plant lore.

Mitchell, Donald D. Kilolani, *Resource Units in Hawaiian Culture.* Honolulu: The Kamehameha Schools Press, 1982.

Prepared as a text for students, this is a highly accessible introduction to many facets of traditional Hawaiian culture. Highly recommended.

Neal, Marie C., *In Honolulu Gardens.* Honolulu: Bernice P. Bishop Museum, 1928.

A survey of the uses and spiritual significance of plants in Hawai'i.

Poire, Napua Stevens, "Night Marchers Scared Her." *Honolulu Advertiser,* October 31, 1971.

A modern account of an encounter with the Night Marchers.

Pukui, Mary Kawena and Samuel H. Elbert, *Hawaiian Dictionary.* Honolulu: University of Hawaii Press, 1986.

> More than a dictionary, this work is filled with detailed information concerning every aspect of life in ancient Hawai'i. A goldmine of traditional lore. This is also the accepted guide to Hawaiian orthography.

Pukui, Mary Kawena, *'Olelo No'eau: Hawaiian Proverbs and Poetical Sayings.* Honolulu: Bishop Museum Press, 1983.

> Over 3,000 sayings collected by Mary Kawena Pukui during a lifetime of work. Reading them, their translations and commentaries, provides an insight into ancient Hawaiian life. A monumental, fascinating, inspirational, humorous, and deeply revealing look at traditional Hawaiian values and beliefs. Indispensable.

Pukui, Mary Kawena, E. W. Haertig, and Catherine A. Lee, *Nana I Ke Kumu (Look To The Source), Volume I.* Honolulu: Hui Hanai, Queen Lili'uokalani Children's Center, 1972.

> Facets of traditional Hawaiian culture and their impact on contemporary Hawaiians. *Mana,* transfiguration of the dead, *akua,* psychic awareness, prophets.

Pukui, Mary Kawena, E. W. Haertig, and Catherine A. Lee, *Nana I Ke Kumu (Look To The Source), Volume II.* Honolulu: Hui Hanai, Queen Lili'uokalani Children's Center, 1972.

> Prayer, sex, childbirth, *kahuna,* and more in old Hawai'i.

Pukui, Mary Kawena, Samuel H. Elbert, and Esther T. Mookini, *Place Names of Hawai'i.* Honolulu: The University Press of Hawaii, 1974.

> A goldmine of information regarding sacred sites throughout Hawai'i. Fascinating reading.

Remy, Jules M., *Contributions of a Venerable Native to the Ancient History of the Hawaiian Islands.* 1874. Reprinted Reno: Outbooks, 1979.

> A short, fascinating document recounting ancient social structure of Hawai'i; *kahuna;* stories of great chiefs.

Shimoda, Jerry Y., "Pu'uhonua-o-Honaunau: Place of Refuge," in *National Parks and Conservation Magazine*. February 1975.

A fine introduction to *pu'uhonua* in general.

Stagner, Ishmael, *Hula!* Laie (O'ahu, Hawai'i): The Institute for Polynesian Studies—Brigham Young University, Hawaii Campus, 1985.

A short, intriguing look at *hula* history and practice, with many splendid photographs.

Sterling, Elspeth P., and Catherine C. Summers, *Sites of Oahu*. Honolulu: Bishop Museum Press, 1988.

Detailed information regarding *heiau*, both extant and vanished, on O'ahu.

St. Lawrence, Sister Mary, *Exploring Nature in Hawaii, Book VII*. Honolulu: The Roman Catholic Diocese of Honolulu, N.D.

Plants, birds, and fish.

Tarallo-Jensen, Lucia and Rocky K. Jensen, *Born the Night of the Gods...When Man Came From Afar*. Honolulu: Anima Gemella Publishers/Hale Naua III, 1989.

This pamphlet, published in conjunction with an exhibit of Rocky Jensen's Hawaiian artwork, greatly relies on the Kumulipo (the best-known Hawaiian genealogical chant) to discuss several *akua* and also some Hawaiian spiritual concepts.

Taylor, Clarice B., *Hawaiian Almanac*. Honolulu: Tongg Publishing, 1957.

A lively collection of short articles on topics ranging from birth omens and Hawaiian medicine to dream lore and love inducement. Mary Kawena Pukui was a major source of information; Clarice B. Taylor was librarian at the Bishop Museum.

Titcomb, Margaret (with the collaboration of Mary Kawena Pukui), *Native Use of Fish in Hawaii*. Honolulu: The University Press of Hawaii, 1972.

Ritual as well as culinary uses of fish are included in this fully illustrated volume.

Uyehara, M. (editor and compiler), *Almanac of Hawaiiana 1969.* Honolulu: Hawaiiana Almanac Publishing Company, 1968.
Hawaiian calendar, birth months, omens, and much else of interest.

Westervelt, William D., *Hawaiian Legends of Ghosts and Ghost-Gods.* 1915. Reprinted Charles E. Tuttle, 1963.
Fascinating accounts of ghosts.

Westervelt, William D., *Hawaiian Legends of Volcanoes.* 1916. Reprinted Rutland (Vermont): Charles E. Tuttle, 1961.
Stories of Pele, Hi'iaka, Kamapua'a, and other *akua,* all centered around volcanic activity.

Index

☽ REACH FOR THE MOON

Llewellyn publishes hundreds of books on your favorite subjects! To get these exciting books, including the ones on the following pages, check your local bookstore or order them directly from Llewellyn.

ORDER BY PHONE
- Call toll-free within the U.S. and Canada, 1-800-THE MOON
- In Minnesota, call (651) 291-1970
- We accept VISA, MasterCard, and American Express

ORDER BY MAIL
- Send the full price of your order (MN residents add 7% sales tax) in U.S. funds, plus postage & handling to:

  Llewellyn Worldwide
  P.O. Box 64383, Dept. K188–0
  St. Paul, MN 55164–0383, U.S.A.

POSTAGE & HANDLING
(For the U.S., Canada, and Mexico)
- $4.00 for orders $15.00 and under
- $5.00 for orders over $15.00
- No charge for orders over $100.00

We ship UPS in the continental United States. We ship standard mail to P.O. boxes. Orders shipped to Alaska, Hawaii, The Virgin Islands, and Puerto Rico are sent first-class mail. Orders shipped to Canada and Mexico are sent surface mail.

International orders: Airmail—add freight equal to price of each book to the total price of order, plus $5.00 for each non-book item (audio tapes, etc.).

Surface mail—Add $1.00 per item.

Allow 2 weeks for delivery on all orders.
Postage and handling rates subject to change.

DISCOUNTS
We offer a 20% discount to group leaders or agents. You must order a minimum of 5 copies of the same book to get our special quantity price.

FREE CATALOG
Get a free copy of our color catalog, *New Worlds of Mind and Spirit*. Subscribe for just $10.00 in the United States and Canada ($30.00 overseas, airmail). Many bookstores carry *New Worlds*—ask for it!

Visit our website at www.llewellyn.com for more information.

WICCA

A Guide for the Solitary Practitioner

SCOTT CUNNINGHAM

Wicca is a book of life, and how to live magically, spiritually, and wholly attuned with Nature. It is a book of sense and common sense, not only about Magick, but about religion and one of the most critical issues of today: how to achieve the much needed and wholesome relationship with our Earth. Cunningham presents Wicca as it is today: a gentle, Earth-oriented religion dedicated to the Goddess and God. This book fulfills a need for a practical guide to solitary Wicca—a need which no previous book has fulfilled.

Here is a positive, practical introduction to the religion of Wicca, designed so that any interested person can learn to practice the religion alone, anywhere in the world. It presents Wicca honestly and clearly, without the pseudo-history that permeates other books. It shows that Wicca is a vital, satisfying part of twentieth century life.

This book presents the theory and practice of Wicca from an individual's perspective. The section on the Standing Stones Book of Shadows contains solitary rituals for the Esbats and Sabbats. This book, based on the author's nearly two decades of Wiccan practice, presents an eclectic picture of various aspects of this religion.

0–87542–118–0
240 pp., 6 x 9, illus., softcover $9.95

To order, call 1-800-THE MOON

Living Wicca

A Further Guide for the Solitary Practitioner

SCOTT CUNNINGHAM

Living Wicca is the long-awaited sequel to Scott Cunningham's wildly successful *Wicca: a Guide for the Solitary Practitioner*. This book is for those who have made the conscious decision to bring their Wiccan spirituality into their everyday lives. It provides solitary practitioners with the tools and added insights that will enable them to blaze their own spiritual paths—to become their own high priests and priestesses.

Living Wicca takes a philosophical look at the questions, practices, and differences within Witchcraft. It covers the various tools of learning available to the practitioner, the importance of secrecy in one's practice, guidelines to performing ritual when ill, magical names, initiation, and the Mysteries. It discusses the benefits of daily prayer and meditation, making offerings to the gods, how to develop a prayerful attitude, and how to perform Wiccan rites when away from home or in emergency situations.

Unlike any other book on the subject, *Living Wicca* is a step-by-step guide to creating your own Wiccan tradition and personal vision of the gods, designing your personal ritual and symbols, developing your own book of shadows, and truly living your Craft.

0–87542–184–9
208 pp., 6 x 9, illus., softcover $12.95

The Complete Book of
Incense, Oils & Brews

Scott Cunningham

For centuries the composition of incenses, the blending of oils, and the mixing of herbs have been used by people to create positive changes in their lives. With this book, the curtains of secrecy have been drawn back, providing you with practical, easy-to-understand information that will allow you to practice these methods of magical cookery.

Scott Cunningham, world-famous expert on magical herbalism, first published *The Magic of Incense, Oils and Brews* in 1986. *The Complete Book of Incense, Oils and Brews* is a revised and expanded version of that book. Scott took readers' suggestions from the first edition and added more than 100 new formulas. Every page has been clarified and rewritten, and new chapters have been added.

There is no special, costly equipment to buy, and ingredients are usually easy to find. The book includes detailed information on a wide variety of herbs, sources for purchasing ingredients, substitutions for hard-to-find herbs, a glossary, and a chapter on creating your own magical recipes.

0–87542–128–8
288 pp., 6 x 9, illus., softcover $12.95

Cunningham's Encyclopedia of Crystals, Gems & Metal Magic
Scott Cunningham

Here you will find the most complete information anywhere on the magical qualities of more than 100 crystals and gemstones as well as several metals. The information for each crystal, gem or metal includes: its related energy, planetary rulership, magical element, deities, Tarot Card, and the magical powers that each is believed to possess. Also included is a complete description of their uses for magical purposes. The classic on the subject.

0–87542–126–1
240 pp., 6 x 9, illus., color plates, softcover $14.95

Cunningham's Encyclopedia of Magical Herbs

SCOTT CUNNINGHAM

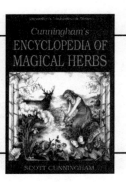

This is the most comprehensive source of herbal data for magical uses ever printed! Almost every one of the over 400 herbs are illustrated, making this a great source for herb identification. For each herb you will also find: magical properties, planetary rulerships, genders, associated deities, folk and Latin names and much more. To make this book even easier to use, it contains a folk name cross reference, and all of the herbs are fully indexed. There is also a large annotated bibliography, and a list of mail order suppliers so you can find the books and herbs you need. Like all of Cunningham's books, this one does not require you to use complicated rituals or expensive magical paraphernalia. Instead, it shares with you the intrinsic powers of the herbs. Thus, you will be able to discover which herbs, by their very nature, can be used for luck, love, success, money, divination, astral projection, safety, psychic self-defense and much more. Besides being interesting and educational it is also fun, and fully illustrated with unusual woodcuts from old herbals. This book has rapidly become the classic in its field. It enhances books such as 777 and is a must for all Wiccans.

0–87542–122–9
336 pp., 6 x 9, illus., softcover $14.95

Earth Power
Techniques of Natural Magic
Scott Cunningham

Magick is the art of working with the forces of Nature to bring about necessary and desiredchanges. The forces of Nature— expressed through Earth, Air, Fire and Water—are our "spiritual ancestors" who paved the way for our emergence from the pre- historic seas of creation. Attuning to and working with these energies in magick not only lends you the power to affect changes in your life, it also allows you to sense your own place in the larger scheme of Nature. Using the "Old Ways" enables you to live a better life and to deepen your understanding of the world. The tools and powers of magick are around you, waiting to be grasped and utilized. This book gives you the means to put Mag- ick into your life, shows you how to make and use the tools, and gives you spells for every purpose.

0–87542–121–0
176 pp., 5¼ x 8, illus., softcover $9.95

Earth, Air, Fire & Water
More Techniques of Natural Magic

SCOTT CUNNINGHAM

A water-smoothed stone . . . The wind . . . A candle's flame . . . A pool of water. These are the age-old tools of natural magic. Born of the Earth, possessing inner power, they await only our touch and intention to bring them to life.

The four Elements are the ancient powerhouses of magic. Using their energies, we can transform ourselves, our lives and our worlds. Tap into the marvelous powers of the natural world with these rites, spells and simple rituals that you can do easily and with a minimum of equipment. *Earth, Air, Fire & Water* includes more than 75 spells, rituals and ceremonies with detailed instructions for designing your own magical spells. This book instills a sense of wonder concerning our planet and our lives; and promotes a natural, positive practice that anyone can successfully perform.

0–897542–131–8
240 pp., 6 x 9, illus., softcover   **$9.95**

Magical Aromatherapy
The Power of Scent

SCOTT CUNNINGHAM

Scent magic has a rich, colorful history. Today, in the shadow of the next century, there is much we can learn from the simple plants that grace our planet. Most have been used for countless centuries. The energies still vibrate within their aromas.

Scott Cunningham has now combined the current knowledge of the physiological and psychological effects of natural fragrances with the ancient art of magical perfumery. In writing this book, he drew on extensive experimentation and observation, research into 4,000 years of written records, and the wisdom of respected aromatherapy practitioners. *Magical Aromatherapy* contains a wealth of practical tables of aromas of the seasons, days of the week, the planets, and zodiac; use of essential oils with crystals; synthetic and genuine oils and hazardous essential oils. It also contains a handy appendix of aromatherapy organizations and distributors of essential oils and dried plant products.

0–87542–129–6
 224 pp., mass market, illus. $3.95

Whispers of the Moon

The Life & Work of
Scott Cunningham, Pagan Prophet

DAVID HARRINGTON &
deTRACI REGULA

Scott Cunningham (b. 1956–d. 1993) authored more than fifty-books in his lifetime, fifteen of which lay the foundation for the non-institutional growth of modern Wicca. For tens of thousands of new Wiccans, their first magic circle was cast using his words of power. In addition, Scott also opened up a new understanding of positive, nature-based magics such as herb, gem and elemental magic.

Whispers of the Moon combines Scott's unfinished autobiography with the added efforts of two of his closest friends. While the book traces his life and growth as a writer as well as a philosopher-magician, it also includes some of Scott's poetry, portions of letters, exposition of his personal philosophy and religion, and the complete text of his self-published pamphlet from 1982: *A Formula Book of Magical Incenses & Oils*.

With remembrances of Scott from many people, this book answers questions about his life, illness and death at age thirty-seven; his involvement in various Wiccan traditions; and his methods of research and discipline as a writer. What's more, it clearly demonstrates his importance as a prophet of modern-day nature religion.

1–56718–559–2
272 pp., 6 x 9, photos, softcover $15.00

To order, call 1-800-THE MOON
Prices subject to change without notice